Philosophers to Astronauts
READER'S THEATER

DEVELOP READING FLUENCY AND TEXT COMPREHENSION SKILLS

Written and Edited by
Alaska Hults

For Helen Black Humbarger

Illustrator: Corbin Hillam
Cover Illustrator: Amy Vangsgard
Designer: Jane Wong-Saunders
Cover Designer: Barbara Peterson
Art Director: Tom Cochrane
Project Director: Carolea Williams

Table of Contents

6 = total number of parts

INTRODUCTION

Fluency instruction provides a bridge between being able to "read" a text and being able to understand it. Readers who decode word by word sound plodding and choppy. They are too busy figuring out the words to think about what they are reading. Fluent readers are accurate, quick, and able to read with expression. They make the reading sound interesting. Beyond the experience of the listener, fluent readers are also demonstrating skills that are crucial to their understanding of what they read. Fluent readers recognize words at a glance, group words into meaningful phrases, and move beyond the struggle to decode individual words. They are able to focus on making sense of what they read.

Reader's Theater is an exciting way to help students improve reading fluency without being too time intensive for the teacher. It requires no props and no additional teaching skills on your part, and it is not difficult to manage. Reader's Theater promotes better reading comprehension because students who have learned to read a passage expressively also come to better understand its meaning. In addition, research says that these gains transfer well to new text. Reader's Theater also addresses standards in listening while providing a fun environment for everyone involved. When students practice their lines, they read and reread the same passages. Under your direction, they gradually add more expression, read more smoothly, and find any subtle meanings in the passages.

The scripts in *Philosophers to Astronauts Reader's Theater* are intended to be read in large groups of 5 to 9 students. Each script is prefaced by an activity that focuses on vocabulary from the script, the factual and fictional background of the piece, fluency instruction specific to that script, and comprehension questions that span the levels of Bloom's Taxonomy. Each script is followed by one or two whole-class activities related to the content of the script.

These scripts are designed for fluency instruction. While they are based on factual information about the time period or characters, many of the characters and scenes are entirely fictional. The overall purpose is to provide students with text at their reading level that is fun to read. The background section that precedes each script provides additional information about the characters or the period around which the script is built. All the scripts provide the following hallmarks of a good Reader's Theater text:

- fast-moving dialogue
- action
- humor
- narrative parts

Philosophers to Astronauts Reader's Theater provides hours of fluency practice that features characters students know and may even admire. The large-group format gives students an opportunity to work together to craft an entertaining reading for a peer or adult audience.

How To Use This Book

Each Reader's Theater script should be covered over the course of five practice days (although those days do not need to be consecutive). The first day should include some or all of the elements of the suggested reading instruction. It should also include an expressive reading by you of the script as students read along silently. On each of the following days, give students an opportunity to practice their reading. On the final day, have each group read its script for the class.

Five sections that support reading instruction precede each script. You will find **vocabulary, background information** for the script, **a brief description of each character,** specific **coaching for fluency instruction,** and **comprehension questions** that progress from the simplest level of understanding to the most complex.

On the first day of instruction, briefly discuss with students the vocabulary. Each vocabulary list includes a short activity to help students understand the meaning of each vocabulary word. For example, the vocabulary activity for Alexander Graham Bell (page 7) asks volunteers to create a chart that teaches the class about one of the words.

Next, use the background and information about each character to tell students what the script will be about and describe the characters.

Read aloud the script, modeling clear enunciation and a storyteller's voice. Do not be afraid to exaggerate your expression—it will hold the attention of your audience and stick more firmly in their minds when they attempt to mimic you later. Model the pacing you expect from them as they read.

Finish the reading instruction by discussing the fluency tips with students and having them answer the questions in the comprehension section.

Now it is time to give students a copy of the script! Use the following schedule of student practice for a five-day instruction period.

Day 1	After following the steps outlined on page 4, give each student a personal copy of the script. Pair students and have Partner A read all the parts on the first page, Partner B read all the parts on the second page, and so on.
Days 2 and 3	Assign students to a group. Give each group a script for each student, and have each student highlight a different part. Have students gather to read aloud the script as many times as time permits. Have them change roles with each reading by exchanging the highlighted scripts. Move from group to group, providing feedback and additional modeling as needed. At the *end* of day 3, assign roles or have students agree on a role to own.

Day 4	Have each group read aloud the script. Move from group to group and provide feedback. Have students discuss their favorite lines at the end of each reading and why the manner in which they are read works well. Repeat.
Day 5	Have each group perform its script for the rest of the class (or other audience members provided by buddy classes and/or school personnel).

Throughout the week, or as time permits, provide students with the activity or activities that follow each script. These are optional and do not have to be completed to provide fluency instruction; however, many provide students with additional background information that may help them better understand the characters or setting of the script.

Additional Tips

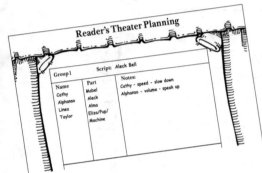

- Use the Reader's Theater Planning reproducible (page 6) to track the assigned roles for each group and to jot down any informal observations you make for assessment. Use these observations to drive future fluency instruction.

- Notice that there are no staging directions in the scripts. These plays are written to be read expressively in a storyteller's voice. If the focus is placed on *acting out* the script, students will shift their focus from the reading to the movement. If students become enchanted with a script and want to act it out, invite them to do so after they have mastered the reading. Then, have the group go through the script and brainstorm their own staging directions to jot in the margins.

- To fit fluency instruction into an already full day of instruction, it will work best to have all groups work on the same script. This will permit you to complete the first day's activities as a whole class. Students will enjoy hearing how another child reads the same lines, and some mild competition to read expressively will only foster additional effort.

- If you have too many roles for the number of students in a group, assign one child more than one part.

- If you have too many students for parts, divide up the narrator parts. As a rule, these parts tend to have longer lines.

- The roles with the greatest and least number of words to read are noted in the teacher pages. The ⬆ and ⬇ indicate a higher or lower *word count*. They are not a reflection of reading level. The narrator parts usually reflect the highest reading level. However, less fluent readers may benefit from having fewer words to master. More advanced readers may benefit from the challenge of the greater word count.

Reader's Theater Planning

Group 1   Script: _____

Name	Part	Notes:

Group 2   Script: _____

Name	Part	Notes:

Group 3   Script: _____

Name	Part	Notes:

Philosophers to Astronauts Reader's Theater © 2004 Creative Teaching Press

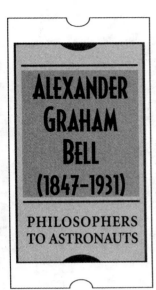

ALEXANDER GRAHAM BELL (1847–1931)

PHILOSOPHERS TO ASTRONAUTS

VOCABULARY

Discuss each of the following words with students. Then, have students choose one of the words to research in a print or an online encyclopedia or dictionary. Have students create a chart that teaches the class more about their word.

affectionate: showing tenderness and care

audience: a group of people gathered to hear something

bellows: a device or piece of equipment with a chamber with flexible sides that can be expanded to draw air in and compressed to force the air out

bypass: to go around

resonates: echoes

torturing (torture): hurting on purpose (e.g., Aleck was *not* torturing his favorite pet.)

vibrating: moving rapidly back and forth or up and down

BACKGROUND

In this play, the children have just returned from seeing a speaking machine at a fair. Alexander Graham Bell really was known as Aleck and he did see the machine at a London exhibit with his father. The entire family was interested in speech, hearing, education of the deaf, and inventing in general. Aleck's uncle and grandfather were known for their talent in speaking. His father was a teacher at a school for deaf students where he met and married Aleck's mother, Elisa.

The dialogue, two neighbor girls, and exact nature of the speaking machine were invented for this play. However, Aleck and his brother did invent such a machine at the urging of their father and Aleck did succeed in manipulating his dog to get it to "talk." The neighbor girl in the play is named Mabel. This was actually the name of his future wife; however, they did not know each other as children in real life. His mother speaks in the play, but in Scotland at the time, she probably used a combination of some spoken words and sign. She really did use an ear tube, and Aleck really did talk from a very young age by speaking directly to her forehead—probably discovered when playing games in her lap as young children do with their mothers. Aleck's family was neither rich nor poor and the house really was full of pianos that everyone in the family played, including his mother.

PARTS

Narrator 1
Narrator 2
Narrator 3
Aleck Bell: 12-year-old boy
*Melville Bell: Aleck's father
*Elisa Bell: Aleck's mother
Melly Bell: 10-year-old brother
*Ed Bell: 16-year-old brother
Mabel: 9-year-old neighbor, girl
Alma: 10-year-old neighbor, girl
*Machine: a talking machine
   made by the boys
*Pup: the dog

*Have one student read the parts
of Elisa, Machine, and Pup. Have a
second student read the parts of
Melville and Ed.

FLUENCY INSTRUCTION

Have students discuss the ages of the characters to help them reflect the maturity level in their reading. When you read aloud the script for students, have them listen for the following:

• In the opening scene, the first speaking character walks into a setting where a deaf woman is playing piano to an empty house. Have students discuss how this would be a rare moment when she could play at a volume that works for her without having to accommodate the needs of her hearing family. Point out that until the character of Elisa knows they are there, all lines will have to be read as if they are spoken over loud music.

• You enunciate very clearly whenever you are speaking for a character who is talking to Elisa. If your character then speaks to one of the other characters, your volume drops and you speak more casually.

• The meaning of a line can change subtly based on the words that are emphasized. Read the line **Aleck:** *Mom is home!* several times, each time emphasizing a different word. Explain that when you emphasize *Mom,* you imply a message about the volume level. When you emphasize *is,* it sounds as if you had perhaps been discussing whether or not she would be home. And when you emphasize *home,* it sounds as if you had been discussing whether she would be in one of a choice of specific places (e.g., the market, a neighbor's house, or home) or perhaps that you were worried she wouldn't be home and are relieved to find that she is.

COMPREHENSION

After you read aloud the script, ask students these questions:

1. What were Aleck and his brother, Melly, trying to invent?
2. From where did they get the idea to build the machine?
3. What were some of the parts the boys needed to build the machine?
4. Why do you think Aleck's father challenged him to make the machine?
5. How do you think having a mother who could not hear influenced Alexander Graham Bell?

ALECK BELL

Philosophers to Astronauts Reader's Theater © 2004 Creative Teaching Press

PARTS

Narrator 1
Narrator 2
Narrator 3
Aleck Bell: 12-year-old boy
Melville Bell: Aleck's father
Elisa Bell: Aleck's mother
Melly Bell: 10-year-old brother
Ed Bell: 16-year-old brother
Mabel: 9-year-old neighbor, girl
Alma: 10-year-old neighbor, girl
Machine: a talking machine
   made by the boys
Pup: the dog

Narrator 1: It is late morning and a woman is sitting in her house in Scotland practicing the piano. The house is mostly empty and she is smiling and relaxed.

Narrator 2: She is playing rather loudly.

Narrator 3: The door bursts open and into the hall rush two boys. They throw their coats on a coatrack.

Aleck: Mom is home!

Melly: What??

Narrator 1: Their father walks in behind them.

Narrator 2: The woman at the piano hits a wrong note.

Aleck and Melly: Oooh . . .

Narrator 3: Mr. Bell sticks his head in the living room and waves his hands to get his wife's attention. She stops playing and picks up a horn that is large and open at one end, small and narrow at the other.

Narrator 1: She sticks the small part in her ear. Melville Bell speaks into it.

Mr. Bell: We had a wonderful time at the show, dear.

Elisa: I thought you would!

Mr. Bell: I have challenged the boys to make a talking machine like the one we saw at the show.

Narrator 2: Aleck bypasses the horn and instead walks up to his mother and speaks just an inch from her forehead. His voice resonates in the bones in her head, and he knows his deaf mother hears him as well as if he spoke in the horn.

ALECK BELL

Narrator 3:	He could speak in the horn, too, but he discovered this method when he was very young, and for them both, it seems more affectionate.
Aleck:	He thinks we cannot do it.
Narrator 1:	Mr. Bell winks at his wife.
Elisa:	I know you can. But you will have to do it with an audience.
Aleck:	What audience?
Elisa:	Mabel and Alma will be over in a few minutes.
Melly:	They will be in the way!
Aleck:	It will be all right, Melly. They are not too bad, for girls. We will be upstairs, Mum!
Melly:	Bye, Mum!
Narrator 2:	Mrs. Bell returns to playing, but now that there are hearing people in the house, she plays softly, tilting her head low to the piano so she can hear the vibrating strings.
Narrator 3:	Upstairs, they find their brother, Ed. He has just finished organizing the workbench that the boys use for their inventions.
Narrator 1:	The entire Bell family is interested in speech and hearing . . .
Narrator 2:	. . . and inventions in general. Aleck has already invented a machine that husks corn. One day he will invent a kind of plane.
Melly:	Oh! This is perfect for the tongue, don't you think?
Narrator 3:	He holds up a strip of leather.
Aleck:	Yes!
Ed:	You aren't going to mess up the room again, are you?
Narrator 1:	Two girls from a nearby farm walk in the room.
Aleck:	You will not believe what we saw today, Mabel!
Melly:	It was a speaking machine! It sounded just like a person, but it was all made of metal and leather and cloth.
Mabel:	What was it for?
Melly and Aleck:	For?

Philosophers to Astronauts Reader's Theater © 2004 Creative Teaching Press

ALECK BELL

Ed: Yes, why was it invented?

Aleck: Oh, who knows? But it was thrilling to hear it!

Melly: It made the hair on your neck stand straight up. That's for sure!

Ed: So you are going to invent one.

Aleck: Father bet us we couldn't.

Mabel: That's all it takes for you. How long do you think it will take?

Aleck: I think we can do it now! Melly already found us a tongue.

Alma: Yuck! Where?

Melly: Not a real tongue, just a strip of leather that can act like one. For example, I make a "t" sound by touching my tongue to my teeth.

Melly and Aleck: Tuh, tuh, tuh.

Alma: Yes, yes, we get it. You can make the leather tongue say "t" by touching it to fake teeth.

Aleck: Good thinking! We need teeth, brother!

Mabel: Puh, puh . . . I guess you need lips, too.

Alma: Huh, huh . . . and some air. And something that makes noise.

Narrator 2:   Aleck picks up another piece of leather lying on the table. He pins it between the top and bottom of both thumbs and blows across it. It vibrates and makes a low "uhhhh" sound.

Mabel: Spooky!

Melly: Perfect!

Narrator 3:   The boys begin to assemble the pieces they have found. With the girls' help, they find items around the house for the teeth, the mouth, and a nose.

Narrator 1:   Melly blows through the back and Aleck moves the tongue.

Machine: Tuh, tuh.

Melly: It is too quiet. We need something that will focus the air better.

Ed: You need a throat for the thing.

Aleck: This piece of paper! We will roll it into a tube like this and tie it closed with this string.

Philosophers to Astronauts Reader's Theater © 2004 Creative Teaching Press

ALECK BELL

Narrator 2: Melly blows hard through the throat. It is only a little louder.

Machine: Tuh, tuh.

Melly: Ooof. It is HARD to blow that much! There must be an easier way.

Aleck: I know! The bellows! Alma, get us the bellows from next to the fireplace there. No, the large one.

Narrator 3: She hands Aleck the bellows. He ties the string so that the end of the throat is tight around the end of the bellows.

Aleck: Pump the bellows hard, Melly.

Machine: Uhhhhhhhhhhh!

All: Yay!!

Aleck: OK, do it again while I move the tongue.

Machine: Tuh, tuh, puh, puh, put, put, thaaaaat, duh, duh, doowwwwnnnn.

Mabel: Put that down! You made it say "Put that down!"

Narrator 1: The dog comes in to investigate the strange noises. Aleck pats the dog on the head and then lifts the small terrier onto the workbench.

Alma: Now what are you doing, Aleck? Torturing the dog?

Narrator 2: Aleck has gently pushed the lips of his Skye terrier into a grin, and using a pencil, moves the patient dog's tongue.

Aleck: No, watch, he likes it . . . speak, Pup!

Narrator 3: The terrier has been trained to growl softly when Aleck says, "Speak!" So he growls. Aleck moves the dog's lips and tongue in the same way he moved the machine's.

Pup: Noooo.

Ed and Melly: Oh! Go get Mother and Father! They have got to see this!

Narrator 1: And so, with the bet won, life continued in the Bell household.

Philosophers to Astronauts Reader's Theater © 2004 Creative Teaching Press

RELATED LESSONS

What Conducts Sound?

OBJECTIVE
Explore the way different materials respond to a tuning fork.

ACTIVITY

In advance, place at a center **tuning forks of various pitches, some books**, a **small tub of water**, and a **rubber block.** (Look for inexpensive science-grade tuning forks through print or online science, music, and medical catalogues.*) Have groups of two to three students visit the center at a time. Give each student a **Sound reproducible (page 14).** Show students how to strike one tip of a tuning fork against the bottom of their shoe to hear its tone. Then, have them place it on each object listed on the reproducible and record their observations. When all students have had a chance to complete the experiment, discuss their observations as a class.

*The best prices found at time of printing were all under $10 each and include www.nursestop.com and www.best-priced-products.com.

The Inventions of Alexander Graham Bell

OBJECTIVE
Gather information about the life of the famous inventor.

ACTIVITY

Give each student a **Bell's Inventions reproducible (page 15).** Review the questions on the bottom of the reproducible, and have students set a purpose for reading. Have students read the paragraphs. Then, divide the class into pairs, and have each pair answer the questions. Discuss the answers as a class.

Answers
1. This piece describes Alexander Graham Bell's plane and hydrofoil.
2. The plane was called the Silver Dart. It was the first Canadian-manned plane to fly. It traveled 40 mph and flew for a full half mile.
3. It was used in World War I to travel on the water and avoid mines.

Sound

Directions: Strike the tuning fork against the bottom of your shoe and listen to the tone it makes. Then place it on the following objects and write what happens to the sound.

Object	What Happens?
table	
water	
book	
rubber block	
your forehead	

What kinds of materials make the tone stop? _____

_____

What kinds of materials make the tone louder? _____

_____

Did any of the materials vibrate in a way that you could see?

Describe what happened. _____

_____

Bell's Inventions

Directions: Read the passage. Answer the questions on a separate piece of paper.

Alexander Graham Bell was the second son of three sons. His mother was an educated deaf woman. His father was an educator of the deaf who taught deaf children to speak and understand spoken words. The men in his family were noted speakers and researchers in speech and hearing. Bell's most famous invention, the telephone, was a result of his interest in sound. But did you know that he also invented a plane and a hydrofoil used in World War I?

Bell's plane was called the Silver Dart. He began developing models of planes in the 1890s—well before the Wright brothers' successful first flight. At the time, many men who worked on developing planes were ridiculed. Bell flew his models in the evening in a small town in Nova Scotia, Canada. In 1907, four years after Orville and Wilbur Wright flew their plane, Bell and his friends flew the Silver Dart. It was the first plane to fly in Canada, and it traveled at 40 mph (64 km) for a full half mile (804 m). At the time, this was very fast and a very long distance for a plane to fly.

Bell invented the hydrofoil while he was working on his plane models. He wanted a way to take off and land on water. Later, when the Unites States entered World War I, he wanted to contribute his efforts to their victory. One problem that the Navy faced was waters full of mines. Bell invented his hydrofoil to skim over the surface of the water, avoid mines, and travel quickly. It reached top speeds of 70 mph (113 km), an incredible speed in 1918.

Alexander Graham Bell's name will always be associated with the telephone, but it was not his only clever and useful invention.

Questions

1. What two inventions of Alexander Graham Bell does this piece describe?
2. List three facts about his airplane.
3. Tell how Bell's hydrofoil was used.

MARIA GAËTANA AGNESI (1718-1799)

PHILOSOPHERS TO ASTRONAUTS

VOCABULARY

Discuss each of the following words with students. Then, have students find each word in the dictionary, copy the definition, and write the guidewords from the dictionary page for that word.

boastful: showing off

drawing room: a slightly formal living room where guests are entertained

manuscript: a written work intended for publication

pianist: someone who plays the piano

presentation: a speech or performance that is meant to teach or communicate ideas

translating: saying the same meaning in a different language

BACKGROUND

Maria Gaëtana Agnesi was the eldest daughter of a wealthy Italian businessman. She was exceptionally precocious and her father took great delight in providing her with excellent tutors from the church. Although she excelled at all of her academic subjects, she was especially gifted at learning languages. By the age of nine, she could speak Latin, Greek, and Hebrew, among others. Her father enjoyed having her demonstrate her talents to visitors. Although she did not particularly enjoy these performances, they were not uncommon at her level of society, and she did not protest doing them for her father. It is known that her sister closest to her in age did attend the event where she recited the Latin argument for including women in the university. The rest is fictionalized. Only Maria and Pietro have their actual names.

Agnesi's father eventually had 21 children, and after his third wife died, Maria took over the education of her younger brothers. She studied mathematics on her own and with the help of an educated monk who was a respected mathematician of the time. Under his guidance and through her gift of being fluent in many languages, she succeeded in translating the work of the mathematicians of her time into one common language (Italian) and in a manner that would help clarify the concepts for students. Although none of the ideas in her math book were original, it was such a remarkable achievement and useful tool that the Pope himself wrote her a letter thanking her for her work. She was named an honorary instructor at the university, although it is unlikely she ever even visited the school. Her life's work was serving the poor and she would eventually die penniless, having given away her inheritance in that endeavor.

Narrator

Pietro Agnesi (Pee-ay-tro):
wealthy Italian businessman

Maria (Mah-ree-ah):
9-year-old girl

Teresa (Ter-ay-sah):
7-year-old sister

Vincenzo (Vin-chen-zoh):
8-year-old brother

Jacopo (Zhah-kah-poe):
6-year-old brother

FLUENCY INSTRUCTION

Have students discuss the ages of the characters to help them reflect the maturity level in their reading. When you read aloud the script for students, have them listen for the following:

• Teresa and Maria are very close in age, but they have very different personalities. Maria is quieter and more serious. Teresa is outgoing and bubbly. Have students listen as you read aloud the top of page 20. Use a faster tempo for the excited Teresa.

• Your voice pauses before a period, especially if the period is before a quote as in **Maria:** *I should just say, "How are you? Isn't the weather grand?" in five languages.*

• Maria, normally a very calm child, does become quite excited at the idea of spending an evening mostly alone with her mother. Remind the class that Maria has many, many brothers and sisters. Model a faster pace and slightly higher volume as Maria responds to her father during this section.

COMPREHENSION

After you read aloud the script, ask students these questions:

1. Is Maria a child or an adult?

2. What is Maria going to present to the visitors?

3. What is unusual about the way in which she will deliver her talk?

4. Why do you think her father was excited about having his eldest daughter show her knowledge to his visitors?

5. Do you think you would have liked to have been like Maria? Explain your answer.

The Performance

Narrator: It is early afternoon and a small group of servants is arranging furniture in the drawing room of a wealthy Italian household into a circle. Children from the household are watching.

Jacopo: Do I have to speak to Father's guests?

Maria: No, Jacopo, don't worry. You just have to be quiet while I'm giving the presentation.

Jacopo: What are you presenting?

Teresa: She's reciting this.

Narrator: Teresa picks up a pile of papers next to Maria and shows them to her brother.

Teresa: See? It's all in Latin.

Vincenzo: Wow! What does it say?

Maria: Um. I do not think you would find it very interesting, Vincenzo. It is about whether or not women should attend the University.

Vincenzo: Women cannot go to the University?

Teresa: Lots of people think they should not, and Maria's paper said they should if they want to.

Vincenzo: Do you think Mother wanted to go to the University?

Maria: You could go ask her.

Vincenzo: Now you are just trying to get rid of me. I'm staying. Soon they will bring in the food!

Jacopo: Why did you decide to write about that? Do you think you will go to the University someday?

THE PERFORMANCE

Maria: I hope not, although it might please Father.

Jacopo: Where do you want to go?

Teresa: I want to travel!

Maria: I thought you wanted to be a pianist?

Teresa: That too. Maybe I can travel and play piano everywhere I go.

Maria: I want to enter the convent.

Jacopo: I would miss you then!

Maria: It wouldn't be for many years, Jacopo. You will be all grown up with business of your own by then.

Vincenzo: So, why did you want to write this paper?

Maria: I didn't really write it. I translated it. My tutor wrote it in Italian. We were sitting around last week trying to find something in the library I hadn't read yet and we could not come up with anything.

Teresa: So as a joke, she grabbed the top page of his manuscript and started translating it aloud in Latin.

Maria: [laughing] Then I did the next paragraph in French.

Teresa: And then she did the third paragraph in Hebrew, just because she knows he isn't as good at that one as she is.

Maria: So he had me copy the entire thing in Latin.

Teresa: It was supposed to be a punishment!

Maria: But I finished the whole thing in one sitting. Father came to check on our progress . . .

Teresa: . . . and when he saw the paper and read it, he knew she had done a particularly good job of translating the tutor's writing.

Maria: [sighing] So he called a few friends for the performance.

Narrator: Three men come walking into the room. They are well dressed. One gentleman is from Italy and the other two are visiting from other European countries. They are men who are very well educated and they have come to see their friend's daughter, who is exceptionally intelligent.

Philosophers to Astronauts Reader's Theater © 2004 Creative Teaching Press

THE PERFORMANCE

Teresa: The guests have arrived already? It must be later than we think!

Maria: Remember, Vincenzo, do not ask for any food unless you are going to eat it.

Teresa: And, Jacopo, no kicking your seat while you are listening to Maria. You must be sure to sit quietly.

Vincenzo and Jacopo: Yes, yes, yes.

Narrator: Their father enters the room, sees the children, and walks towards them.

Pietro: Children!

Children: Hello, Father!

Pietro: Has the food arrived yet?

Jacopo: No, and I have been waiting and waiting!

Pietro: Why don't you run over to the kitchen and see if cook needs any help bringing the food over.

Jacopo: I will do that!

Narrator: The boy trots out of the room.

Pietro: Are you ready, Maria?

Maria: Yes.

Pietro: Nervous? You don't need to be!

Maria: I am not nervous. I just feel bad for the men who come and listen and do not find my presentation very interesting.

Pietro: What are you talking about? They only come to hear you!

Maria: They come to see the girl who can speak five languages. I should just say, "How are you? Isn't the weather grand?" in five languages.

Pietro: You should be proud of your talents! Besides, it would not work to do it that way. They would think I had just taught you those two sentences in five languages.

Maria: It just seems boastful to show off like this.

Pietro: You should be very proud! And anyway, think about the material you are presenting here today. It is true that some of these men really do not believe that women can be their intellectual equal.

Philosophers to Astronauts Reader's Theater © 2004 Creative Teaching Press

THE PERFORMANCE

Maria: How am I helping then?

Pietro: Because, my eldest and firstborn child, you are more intelligent than most of the men in this room.

Teresa: I know it is not my paper to recite, but even if you do not want the freedom to attend college for yourself, you may want it for your daughter.

Maria: Or for my sister . . .

Pietro: I just want you to be proud of what you can do.

Maria: I want to do more to help people who cannot help themselves, not to educate men who are already educated!

Pietro: Then convince these men that your argument is sound, by performing in perfect Latin, and you will have helped the intelligent women who want to take University classes and cannot be here this afternoon to speak for themselves.

Maria: Father, that's not what I mean. I want to feed and clothe the poor.

Pietro: I know what you mean, but you know this is important to me. Finish your performance this afternoon and then as a reward I will let you attend a theater performance with your mother.

Maria: No other children?!?

Pietro: Except the baby. Mother will take the baby of course.

Maria: Yes, yes, of course the baby. Thank you, Father! I would like that very much.

Vincenzo: Lucky you! What can I do to earn an evening with Mother!

Pietro: You can sit by your brother during the reading and help him remember to sit still and not whisper.

Vincenzo: Deal!

Pietro: Teresa, thank you for helping your sister practice. I know she benefits from your company.

Teresa: Here comes Jacopo and the food! I will help set up. Maria, you should get ready. Vincenzo and Jacopo, it is time to find a seat at the back.

All: Let us go, then! It is time to begin!

Philosophers to Astronauts Reader's Theater © 2004 Creative Teaching Press

RELATED LESSONS

Math Dictionary

OBJECTIVE

Define mathematical concepts and review common math concepts.

ACTIVITY

Give each student a **math textbook with glossary, drawing paper,** and **crayons or markers.** Give each student a **Math Concepts reproducible (page 23),** have students choose a concept to illustrate and describe or define, or assign each concept to a student. Have students write at the top of their drawing paper the name of the concept and at the bottom, a definition or description of the concept. Then, in the center of the paper, have them illustrate the concept. Bind finished papers in a Class Math Dictionary.

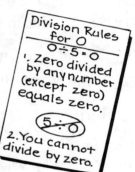

Greek and Latin Roots

OBJECTIVE

Match words with Greek and Latin roots to their root.

ACTIVITY

Give each student a **Greek and Latin Root Words reproducible (page 24).** Read aloud each root and review its meanings with students. Then, read aloud the words in the word bank. Have students discuss the meaning of each root word. You may choose to have less fluent readers copy the word from the word bank to the column below the appropriate root word immediately, or have more fluent readers do so after you have discussed all of the word meanings.

ANSWERS

auto = self   automatic, automobile, autograph

aqua = water   aquifer, aquatic, aquamarine

geo = earth   geometry, geologist, geography

cogn = know   incognito, cognizant, cognition

Math Concepts

Directions: Choose a math concept to define or describe and illustrate on drawing paper.

Multiplication factor product **Division** divisor dividend quotient rules for 0 rules for 1 **Addition** addend sum **Subtraction** difference subtrahend **Fractions** equivalent fractions adding like fractions	**Graphs** bar graph line graph circle graph pictograph **Measurement** length weight capacity geometry closed figure open figure line segment angles (vertex, side) angles (types) congruent figures symmetrical figures perimeter area plane figures solid figures

Philosophers to Astronauts Reader's Theater © 2004 Creative Teaching Press

Greek and Latin Root Words

Directions: Greek and Latin were once considered the core curriculum for a good education. Today, studying these languages is a quick way to improve your own vocabulary and grammar. Match the words in the word box to their Greek and Latin roots. Write each word under the correct heading.

Word Bank			
automobile aquifer cognizant	aquamarine cognition geologist	geography autograph aquatic	incognito geometry automatic

Greek	Latin
auto = self	aqua = water
geo = earth	cogn = know

Philosophers to Astronauts Reader's Theater © 2004 Creative Teaching Press

THOMAS EDISON (1847–1931)

PHILOSOPHERS TO ASTRONAUTS

VOCABULARY

Discuss each of the following words with students. Then, have students choose one of the words to define and illustrate.

acceptable: all right

extraordinarily: very unusual

grounded: to lose household privileges

muffled: heard through a heavy material, indistinct

youngest: in a group of people—the person born most recently

BACKGROUND

Thomas Edison's mother, who had once been a trained teacher, home schooled him. He attended public school briefly, but he was a poor student who didn't seem to be able to focus on the lesson or sit still. Under his mother's watchful eye, however, he flourished.

Either as a result of childhood illness or because of a blow to the head (from an angry train employee when he snuck part of his laboratory on board the train), Edison was mostly deaf by the time he was in his late teens. He seemed to benefit from the loss of his hearing by becoming even more focused on his work.

He turned his training as a telegraph operator into the opportunity to travel and find new jobs. Eventually, he was well paid for a stock-ticker invention and he used this money to finance future inventions. He would go on to register more patents than any other single human being.

In this story, his basement laboratory is accurately depicted. Harriet's age is estimated. The playmate and scene are fictitious.

PARTS

Narrator 1
Narrator 2
Thomas: 12-year-old boy
Mrs. Edison: Thomas's mother
Mr. Edison: Thomas's father
Harriet Stole: Thomas's grown-up sister
Charles: 12-year-old neighbor

FLUENCY INSTRUCTION

Have students discuss the ages of the characters to help them reflect the maturity level in their reading. When you read aloud the script for students, have them listen for the following:

• The volume decreases to show that someone is speaking from a distance or speaking in a small space. Have students name at least one place where characters would talk more quietly. Model for students a "stage whisper." Point out that the characters cannot really whisper or the audience will not hear them.

• Enunciating words very slowly and clearly is another way to show anger. Demonstrate this with the line **Mr. Edison:** *Absolutely not. No access to your lab for two weeks.*

• You pause to show thought as Thomas realizes that he cannot work in his lab because he has been grounded from it in the line **Thomas:** *I can't. I am busy with a project in the . . . oh. I guess I can then.*

COMPREHENSION

After you read aloud the script, ask students these questions:

1. Where is Thomas working at the start of the script?

2. What is the loud bang?

3. How does Mrs. Edison show she understands what is happening in her basement?

4. What was the reason Thomas was grounded?

5. Do you think that Thomas's parents ever worried about what Thomas was doing? Explain your answer.

BOOM!

PARTS

Narrator 1
Narrator 2
Thomas: 12-year-old boy
Mrs. Edison: Thomas's mother
Mr. Edison: Thomas's father
Harriet Stole: Thomas's grown-up
    sister
Charles: 12-year-old neighbor

Narrator 1: It is early afternoon and a woman is rolling out pie crust in the kitchen of an old farmhouse in Michigan.

Narrator 2: There is an extraordinarily loud bang from below. She slams down the rolling pin.

Mrs. Edison: Thomas Alva Edison! What was that?!?

Narrator 1: The reply is muffled as it comes through the basement door.

Thomas: Nothing, Mom! Don't worry!

Narrator 2: Mrs. Edison washes the flour off her hands. She knows her youngest son well. It is time to check on his work.

Mrs. Edison: Oh, my, what is that smell?

Narrator: A terrible odor comes through the door, and with it, smoke.

Mrs. Edison: Thomas!! That does not smell like nothing!

Thomas: Shucks . . . Mom, could you bring a bucket?

Narrator 1: Mrs. Edison grabs a bucket that is half-filled with water. It is sitting by the top of the stairs as if this is not the first time that a fire has started in the basement laboratory.

Narrator 2: She opens the door and sees smoke everywhere.

Narrator 1: At that point, Thomas runs up the stairs. He takes the bucket and closes the door behind him.

Thomas: Um. We should let it air out down there, Mom.

Narrator 2: His father and sister walk into the kitchen.

Harriet: What is that awful smell? Did you burn something, Mama?

Mrs. Edison: When was the last time I burnt something, Harriet?

Harriet: Oh, it's Thomas again.

Philosophers to Astronauts Reader's Theater © 2004 Creative Teaching Press

Thomas: What? It has been, about, oh . . .

Mr. Edison: Three weeks. And what did I tell you the last time?

Thomas: No! It has been at least two months!

Harriet: You have your head in the clouds again, Thomas. It was three weeks ago exactly, since I only come home for dinner on Wednesday night, and the whole house smelled exactly like this.

Thomas: Not exactly. One of the chemicals is different.

Mr. Edison: They are opening a new public school here in town, you know.

Harriet: Oh really? Are you going to send Thomas?

Mrs. Edison: Here we go again.

Mr. Edison: We have not decided. I say it would be good for him. Your mother says it just won't work out.

Mrs. Edison: We have tried formal school for him twice before. He can't hear with all the other kids around and the teacher ends up getting mad that he won't answer the question.

Mr. Edison: The teacher gets mad because he asks too many questions!

Mrs. Edison: What kind of school won't let you ask questions?

Harriet: Never mind. I shouldn't have brought it up. Mother, you are doing a fine job educating him.

Mrs. Edison: Thank you.

Harriet: But, Thomas, you must be more careful. You could burn down mother and father's house!

Thomas: I am being careful! I just happened to knock my elbow . . .

Narrator 1:   He is interrupted by another loud bang. And another . . .

Thomas: OK, I will be back in a minute.

Mr. Edison: Where is that bucket?

Narrator 2:   Thomas and his father run down the stairs. There is another loud bang, followed by a yell from his father.

Mr. Edison: What is all this stuff?

BOOM!

Thomas: It is just an experiment I am working on with some rubber.

Mr. Edison: Is that all the smoke?

Thomas: No, I don't think so. I think I burned all the rubber up already.

Mr. Edison: I found the fire!

Thomas: There, that is it. It is out.

Narrator 1: Back in the kitchen, another boy enters.

Charles: Hi, Mrs. Edison! Hi, Mrs. Stole!

Harriet and Mrs. Edison: Hi, Charles.

Charles: Is Thomas here?

Mrs. Edison: He is in the basement somewhere.

Harriet: Wait just a bit, Charles. I would not go down there.

Mr. Edison: That is it, son! I am sorry to do this but you are grounded for two weeks!

Thomas: Grounded?

Mr. Edison: Absolutely no privileges at all.

Charles: Oh, he probably can't play in the ball game then?

Thomas: Dad!!

Mr. Edison: There is no changing my mind. If you cannot think ahead about what you are doing and assure me that my house will not burn down around my ears, then you need a break from your studies.

Thomas: Father, please, I have really been making some progress here!

Charles: What are they talking about?

Harriet: One of his experiments.

Narrator 2: Thomas and Mr. Edison come back up the stairs. They enter the kitchen, covered in soot.

Mr. Edison: Absolutely not. No access to your lab for two weeks.

Mrs. Edison: You heard him, Thomas. I am sorry to see your project interrupted, but two fires in one month is just not acceptable.

Thomas: What will I do for two weeks?

Philosophers to Astronauts Reader's Theater © 2004 Creative Teaching Press

Mr. Edison: You can do chores, you can help your mother, you can sell extra papers for your job on the railroad!

Mrs. Edison: The shed needs whitewashing.

Mr. Edison: There, you can do that. And when all of your work is done, you can play ball with the neighbor kids. You do not do nearly enough of that, always holed-up in your lab.

Thomas: Charles, tell him, I am awful at ball.

Charles: I wouldn't say awful, exactly . . .

Thomas: I cannot hit the ball. I cannot throw the ball where it ought to go. The other day I nearly flattened Junior Jones trying to throw the ball to third!

Charles: You are a pretty fair umpire though. That's what I came by for. We need someone to call for us at tonight's game.

Thomas: I can't. I am busy with a project in the . . . oh. I guess I can then.

Harriet: You do not need to hear well for that?

Thomas: Honestly, Harriet. You do not need to hear well for a lot of things in life.

Harriet: You do not need to be a smart aleck, Thomas.

Thomas: No, it actually helps to not be distracted by the people watching the game.

Charles: Thomas is the only umpire who doesn't get bothered by the hecklers.

Thomas: I can't hear them in the crowd.

Mrs. Edison: That sounds nice, dear. I wasn't aware you had been playing ball recently at all.

Thomas: I don't play unless I am the umpire.

Mr. Edison: You can't get any better at the game if you do not try the other positions, son!

Charles: No offense, Mr. Edison, but I do not think anyone could get any worse at the game than Thomas.

Thomas: Some friend you are.

Charles: Just helping him understand. You ARE a fine umpire.

Mr. Edison: And grounded from your lab. So, go play ball.

Narrator 1: Mr. Edison goes back down the stairs to open the basement doors to let out the smoke.

Philosophers to Astronauts Reader's Theater © 2004 Creative Teaching Press

RELATED LESSONS

Let There Be Light

OBJECTIVE

Gather information about two types of lightbulbs.

ACTIVITY

Give each student a **Let There Be Light reproducible (page 32).** Review the questions on the bottom of the reproducible, and have students set a purpose for reading. Have students read the paragraphs. Then, divide the class into pairs, and have each pair answer the questions. Discuss the answers as a class.

ANSWERS

1. The two types of light discussed are incandescent and fluorescent.
2. Incandescent bulbs get very hot and can burn you.
3. Fluorescent bulbs use less energy.

Which Light?

OBJECTIVE

Compare incandescent and fluorescent lightbulbs.

ACTIVITY

Divide the class into small groups, and give each group a **Venn Diagram (page 33).** Have students use the **Let There Be Light reproducible (page 32)** to fill in the characteristics of incandescent and fluorescent lights. Then, have the class discuss the ways in which the two types of lightbulbs are similar and different.

Name_____   Date _____

Let There Be Light

Directions: Read the passage. Answer the questions on a separate piece of paper.

An incandescent lightbulb has a small wire called a filament inside. The filament is a very thin and long wire that is coiled inside the glass case. Light is given off when electricity heats this filament to very high temperatures. In addition to the light, heat is also given off. After being on for a few minutes, the lightbulb is hot and cannot be touched. These lights can be used both inside and outside.

A fluorescent lightbulb is a tube that is filled with gas and has an electrode at each end. The tube uses electricity to heat the gas to produce ultraviolet light. This ultraviolet light is changed to the light we use by a chemical on the inside of the glass tube. While some heat is produced in this process, it is low and you can touch the tube. The fluorescent lightbulb works best at room temperatures and is usually only used inside.

Both types of lightbulbs can be used in our homes and schools. Many schools and businesses use fluorescent lights because they are more energy efficient. This means it costs less money to light a room with them.

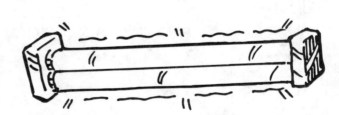

Questions

1. What two types of light are discussed in the article?

2. Why is it a bad idea to touch an incandescent lightbulb?

3. Why are fluorescent bulbs popular in schools and businesses?

Philosophers to Astronauts Reader's Theater © 2004 Creative Teaching Press

Venn Diagram

Directions: Use the Let There Be Light page to fill in the Venn diagram.

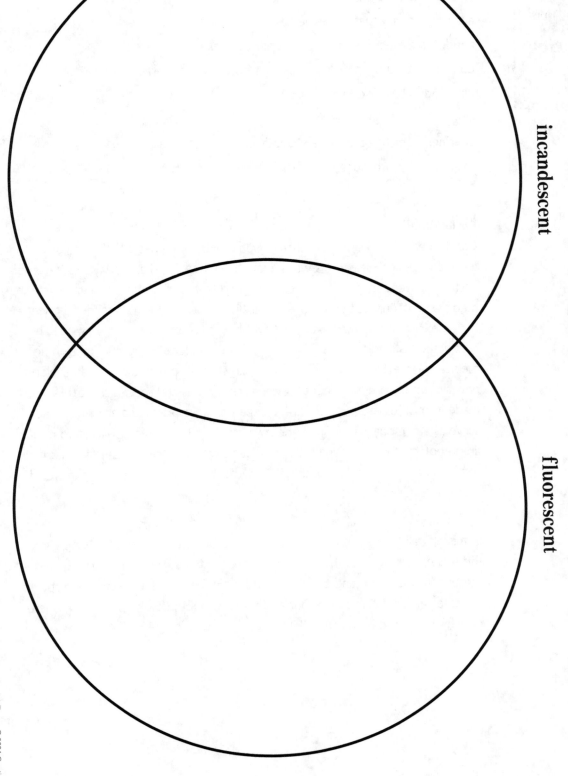

incandescent

fluorescent

CARL LINNAEUS (1707–1778)

PHILOSOPHERS TO ASTRONAUTS

VOCABULARY

Discuss each of the following words with students. Then, have volunteers pantomime the meaning of each word.

accuse: to say that someone has done something wrong or illegal

antidote: a medicine that works against the effects of a poison

compare: to study in order to find out how things are alike and different

dirt clod: a ball or clump of dirt, often damp

fling: to throw carelessly

peering: looking hard or very closely, especially at details

shove: to push along or forward from behind

BACKGROUND

Carl Linneaus was born in southern Sweden. His father was a Lutheran pastor and an avid gardener. His parents were disappointed that he did not want to become a pastor but were encouraged when it seemed that Carl would pursue a degree in medicine. The university he chose actually had a fairly poor medical department but an excellent botany department, which was his preference anyway. After he completed his studies there, he did transfer to a different university to earn his medical degree. He spent the rest of his life studying plants and would develop a new system for ordering species, giving each a genus and species name. His system made it much easier to classify and compare various plants and animals. Carl did serve as a personal physician to the royal family, but his most significant contributions are in botany. It is interesting to know that he was an excellent Latin scholar. If his passion had been Greek, would the classification system used around the world today be in Greek?

In this play, all the names are accurate, except for that of Nina, who was created for this scene. The events in the scene are entirely fictional. There are a variety of nettles throughout the world and the one described in the play does grow in Europe. Its antidote is a plant called dock, but it is not known if these plants grew anywhere near his childhood home.

PARTS

Narrator 1
Narrator 2
Narrator 3
Carl: 12-year old boy
Christina Linnaeus:
    Carl's mother
Nils Linnaeus: Carl's father
Nina: 12-year-old cousin

FLUENCY INSTRUCTION

Have students discuss the ages of the characters to help them reflect the maturity level in their reading. When you read aloud the script for students, have them listen for the following:

- The pace of the reading helps communicate the personality of the character. Point out that Nina, always in a rush, speaks as rapidly as she moves. Carl, who moves at an unhurried pace, speaks more slowly.
- The pace slows down when someone is anxious or worried. Have students name two characters who are anxious or worried at some point in the story.
- When Carl is thinking through a problem, his pace slows down. Have students name two places where Carl is thinking aloud.
- Your voice modulates more for emphasis when you express frustration as in the line *Christina: Oh, dear, and I just washed these towels.*
- Your voice pauses at a period as in the line **Nils:** *It's four pages. How long will that take you?*

COMPREHENSION

After you read aloud the script, ask students these questions:

1. What is Carl reading at the start of the scene?

2. What kind of work does Carl's father do?

3. How would you describe the character of Carl? Nina?

4. If someone said you were like the character of Nina, would you be insulted or complimented? Why?

5. Do you think that Carl Linneaus and Thomas Edison would get along? Linneaus and Maria Gaëtana Agnesi? Explain your answers.

NETTLESOME

PARTS

Narrator 1
Narrator 2
Narrator 3
Carl: 12-year old boy
Christina Linnaeus:
  Carl's mother
Nils Linnaeus: Carl's father
Nina: 12-year-old cousin

Narrator 1: It is late in the morning and a boy is sitting in his family's kitchen at a small table near the window. He is holding a small flower, looking carefully at it, and then peering at the illustrations in a book.

Narrator 2: Every few minutes he turns a page and continues to compare the flower to the pictures.

Carl: This is silly. There has got to be a better way to organize the plants.

Christina: What are you doing, son? Your father is looking for you.

Narrator 3: The boy's mother has entered the kitchen. She has an armful of freshly folded towels.

Carl: I found a new plant in your garden. I don't know what it is, so I'm looking it up.

Christina: Another weed? I hope you pulled it all up and by the roots!

Carl: No, I wanted to see how quickly it grows.

Christina: Pull it out of my garden, Carl. It doesn't matter how quickly it grows if it crowds out my new peas.

Carl: I will do it tomorrow, Mom.

Narrator 1: There are footsteps pounding in the hallway. Out of breath, a young girl flings herself through the door.

Nina: Carl! I've been looking for you everywhere!

Carl: Nina! You are getting mud all over the floor!

Nina: What? Oh, sorry about that. Look!

Narrator 2: She shoves a fistful of something in his face. Dirt clods go flying.

Carl: At your dirty hands? I have seen those before. Oh! There's a pill bug on your thumb.

Nina: What? Oh, right. Pill bug.

Philosophers to Astronauts Reader's Theater © 2004 Creative Teaching Press

NETTLESOME

Narrator 3: She flicks it off.

Christina: Nina, dear, we do not flick bugs onto the floor.

Nina: Sorry, auntie. So what do you think, Carl?

Carl: About what?

Nina: About the flowers, cousin? What are they?

Carl: Since when do you care about flowers, Nina? Other than the ones growing out of your ears, you can't possibly stop long enough to smell them!

Narrator 1: Nina points to her arm.

Nina: Since they made my arm do this . . .

Narrator 2: There is a red, raised rash all up her arm.

Carl: Nina!! Get that out of my face!

Nina: Oh! Do you think it's contagious?

Narrator 3: She scratches the rash thoughtfully, not looking the least bit concerned.

Narrator 1: Carl gets up to fetch a broom.

Carl: No, I think you found a patch of stinging nettle and I think you have wrongly accused that bunch of wild grass you are flinging around my mother's clean kitchen.

Nina: Oh, really? What does nettle look like? The only plants there were this grassy stuff and a plant with fuzzy leaves.

Carl: Right. It was the fuzzy plant. You touch it and the fuzz is really thousands of tiny needles that imbed themselves in your skin. It is a kind of nettle.

Narrator 2: Nina is still scratching. She stops to look thoughtfully at her arm.

Nina: Actually, Carl, it really hurts. What do I do?

Christina: Oh, Nina, honestly. Let me look at it.

Carl: The sting should go away pretty soon. It might help to rub some dock on it. You can also use the juice of the actual nettle plant, but that takes longer as it works best when you soak it awhile.

Nina: I think my arm is on fire.

Philosophers to Astronauts Reader's Theater © 2004 Creative Teaching Press

NETTLESOME

Christina: Do we have any of that dock plant?

Carl: I haven't seen any around.

Narrator 3: A tall, slender man enters the kitchen. He is reading from a bible and muttering to himself. He notices his son.

Nils: There you are! I was looking for you everywhere.

Carl: We are trying to help Nina with her arm. Mom, let's try just dipping a cloth in really cold water and applying that to her arm.

Christina: Oh, dear, and I just washed these towels.

Narrator 1: She leaves to go find cold water.

Nils: It looks as if the girl could use a bath anyway . . .

Nina: Uncle! Ow! Don't touch it.

Nils: Carl, I want you to read this piece I found and translate it for me. I think it might be an interesting bit for this Sunday's sermon.

Narrator 2: Christina returns with the cold, wet towel. She hands it to Nina who places it on her arm.

Carl: You're dripping.

Nils: Carl, the Latin piece?

Carl: Oh, right. How long is it? I still have three pages I have to translate tonight for school tomorrow.

Nils: It's four pages. How long will that take you?

Nina: Four pages of Latin? I would die!

Carl: Just because it's four pages doesn't necessarily mean it is hard. It all depends.

Nina: Depends on what, how boring it is?

Carl: Just because it is written in a foreign language does not mean it can't be funny, Nina.

Nils: Of course, I don't usually have much use for humorous articles.

Nina: I could find you some, uncle! I read a very funny book last week!

Nils: I am sure you did, niece, but I have parishioners to tend to and not much time for that sort of thing.

Philosophers to Astronauts Reader's Theater © 2004 Creative Teaching Press

NETTLESOME

Carl: Let me see the article.

Nils: Do your homework first, then, if you have time, look at the article for me.

Christina: How is your arm, dear?

Narrator 3: Nina peeks under the towel.

Nina: Oh, it is looking better. Is there any more cold water? I think I'm warming the towel.

Nils: Oh, my! That is red! Can you offer her anything better than the towel?

Carl: Is it still on fire? I can go look for some dock or start soaking the nettle for an antidote.

Nina: Anti-what?

Carl: Antidote. Something that works against the poison in the nettle.

Nina: Oh, please, cousin? I promise not to tease you anymore about your Latin or book reading or plants.

Narrator 1: Carl takes the papers from his father and places them on the kitchen table. He heads out the back door.

Christina: Does your mother know you're here, dear?

Nina: Of course! As soon as I told her a plant had done it, she sent me over to see Carl.

Nils: He will never make much of a minister, Christina. Perhaps we should encourage him to become a physician!

Christina: What a good idea, Nils. We will ask around to find a good university for him after he is done with his Latin education.

Narrator 2: Carl returns with a handful of leaves. He hands them to Nina.

Carl: Try rubbing the light side against your arm.

Nina: Like this? Oh! Wow! That really helps!

Narrator 3: Carl's father and mother nod thoughtfully. Nina sighs with relief.

RELATED LESSONS

Fish Sort

OBJECTIVE

Create a classification chart to identify imaginary fish.

ACTIVITY

Give each student a **large sheet of construction paper** and three **Imaginary Fish reproducibles (page 41).** Have students cut out the fish from the first reproducible and sort them into two main groups by any characteristic they choose. Explain that the attribute they sort by at this level must not exclude any of the fish. Tell students these are their two main sets. Then, have them cut out the second page and sort their two sets into four subsets. If they are able to, have them cut out the third reproducible and further sort the subsets into two additional groups each. Then, have students glue their sets and subsets on a large piece of construction paper and label each group with its identifying characteristic.

What Is the Name?

OBJECTIVE

Gather information about Carl Linnaeus.

ACTIVITY

Give each student a **What Is the Name? reproducible (page 42).** Review the questions on the bottom of the reproducible, and have students set a purpose for reading. Have students read the paragraphs. Then, divide the class into pairs, and have each pair answer the questions. Discuss the answers as a class.

ANSWERS

1. Two naturalists could talk about the same plant and not know it.
2. The characteristics of a plant help you find its genus.
3. Linnaeus's system is still important today because a plant or an animal can still have many common names. The use of scientific names helps get rid of the confusion.

Imaginary Fish

Directions: Cut out the fish. Sort them by characteristics. Then, glue them to a large piece of construction paper and write a short description of each set of fish.

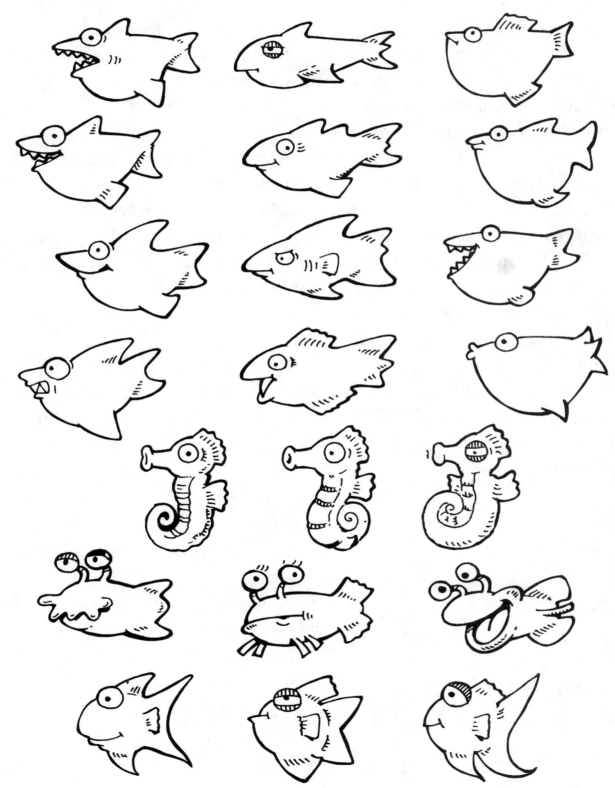

What Is the Name?

Directions: Read the passage. Answer the questions on a separate piece of paper.

Before Carl Linnaeus, most naturalists gave very long Latin names to plants. One naturalist might give a plant one name and another naturalist would give it a different name. This was confusing. With that system of plant names, two naturalists could be talking about the same plant and not even know it. Plus, the common names were different from the Latin names.

Linnaeus's classification system had many groups and each plant could be matched to a specific group. He used the characteristics of a plant such as the shape of the petals or the kind of seeds to decide which group it fit. Each group had a Latin name. This name is called a genus. Each plant had its own species name. The whole name for the plant is its genus and species name. While there were still different common names for a plant, the two-word Latin name is always the same. Now, when naturalists talk about a plant, they know that they are talking about the same plant.

Today, we still use the same system that Linnaeus developed. It is used for both plants and animals. Plants and animals may still have a variety of common names. The puma, the mountain lion, the cougar, and the panther are the same animal, Felis concolor. The tulip tree and yellow popular are both the same tree, Liriodendron tulipifera.

Questions
1. What was the problem with the old way of naming plants?
2. How do the characteristics of a plant help determine its scientific name?
3. Why is Linnaeus's system still important today?

Philosophers to Astronauts Reader's Theater © 2004 Creative Teaching Press

CHARLES DARWIN (1809–1882)

PHILOSOPHERS TO ASTRONAUTS

VOCABULARY

Discuss each of the following words with students. Then, have students discuss why each word might be important to understanding the script.

adapt: to change something to meet a given set of requirements

cribbage: a card game in which the score is kept by moving pegs along rows of holes in a small board

frankly: speaking plainly; not attempting to be diplomatic or excessively polite

jibbering: to talk nonsense

shish kebob: a dish of marinated meat and vegetables barbequed on a skewer

BACKGROUND

Charles Darwin developed the theory of natural selection. He was also what some would call a late bloomer. He possessed no great talents as a child. He was considered an uninspired student and was more interested in dogs and fishing than his studies. His father finally removed him from his boarding school when he was 16 for not making good use of the opportunity. Still, he did enroll at the University of Edinburgh, and there, through a series of unrelated events, he developed an interest in natural science. He learned taxidermy there, which gave him a much deeper understanding of animal anatomy. He read books on natural science, joined a science club with an interest in studying nature, and gained a mentor in the form of one of his professors. Nevertheless, he once again succeeded in getting himself pulled from school by his father for not working hard enough on his studies.

Now seriously concerned that his youngest son would never amount to much, his father sent him to Cambridge University to study for the clergy. He was *still* a miserable student, barely attending enough lectures to stay enrolled. (It should be noted, however, that he scored well on exams. He was tenth in his class on the final exam.) However, he studied natural science on his own there and after three years had a fairly strong understanding of natural sciences. It was through his mentor there, Professor Reverend John Henslow, that he gained experience as a scientist and made the connections that would enable him to pursue a study of the natural world.

In this story, Charles Darwin is playing a game of cards with friends from the *Beagle*. All names and characters except his are fictional. There may not have been a reverend on board the *Beagle*, but the boat did exist. It was a British survey ship, and Darwin was its unpaid naturalist. Erasmus was actually the name of his brother.

PARTS

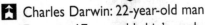

Narrator

Charles Darwin: 22-year-old man

Erasmus: 17-year-old ship's cook

Thomas: 15-year-old errand boy

Reverend: 30-year-old
ship's reverend

Doc: 28-year-old ship's doctor

Note: The Reverend, Doc, and
Thomas have parts of equal
length. There are no lower
word counts for this script.

FLUENCY INSTRUCTION

Have students discuss the ages of the characters to help them reflect the maturity level in their reading. When you read aloud the script for students, have them listen for the following:

- Erasmus likes Charles. He shows that by participating earnestly in the conversation in lines like *Erasmus: And the short, round beak could not get inside the cracks of the tree bark!* But Erasmus also enjoys teasing Charles, as is apparent in lines such as *Erasmus: Of course not! What kind of life is that? Charles, you need to develop some skills. Your education is wasted.* Point out that Erasmus would show the laughter in his voice when he is kidding in order to avoid actually hurting Charles's feelings.

- Point out that the reverend is held in high esteem by the other members of the crew. Have students find two lines that demonstrate this.

- Your voice pauses when your character stops talking to one person and starts talking to another as in the lines *Charles: Stop jibbering and play your hand, Erasmus. The bird eats with its beak. Assuming it has not been caught by a ship's cook, anyway.* In this example, the first sentence is addressed to Erasmus and the remaining sentences are for the other crew members.

COMPREHENSION

After you read aloud the script, ask students these questions:

1. Where does the scene take place?

2. Which characters are the eldest? Which are the youngest?

3. Describe what happens in the scene.

4. What is the reason Charles is interested in the birds and turtles?

5. The *Beagle* was a survey ship. Its mission was to plot the position of various land-masses and collect information about them for mapmaking. Why do you think a naturalist might have been helpful on such a ship?

THE BIRDS

Philosophers to Astronauts Reader's Theater © 2004 Creative Teaching Press

PARTS

Narrator
Charles Darwin: 22-year-old man
Erasmus: 17-year-old ship's cook
Thomas: 15-year-old errand boy
Reverend: 30-year-old
  ship's reverend
Doc: 28-year-old ship's doctor

Narrator: It is early afternoon and a small group of men are sitting down to play cards. They sit cross-legged in a circle on deck of a large English ship known as the H.M.S. *Beagle*. The ship's doctor shuffles the cards.

Doc: What are we playing, then? I need to know how many cards to deal out.

Erasmus: How about a couple of hands of poker?

Charles and Thomas: Erasmus!

Erasmus: Not a good idea?

Thomas: [almost whispering] You cannot play poker with a reverend!

Erasmus: Oh! Pardon me, Reverend. I forgot myself.

Reverend: How about a simple game of Crazy Eights?

Charles and Erasmus: Not again!

Doc: Canasta?

Thomas: What's that?

Charles: How about cribbage?

Others: [taking turns, overlapping] Yes. OK. Yes, that's fine.

Thomas: I will go get the cribbage board.

Narrator: The young man hurries off.

Doc: So, Charles, did you see anything interesting on the island yesterday?

Charles: I found four turtles and eight finches.

Reverend: You seem to find a lot of birds and turtles.

Charles: There are plenty of them on every island, and each is different in some small way.

Reverend: How are they different? Are they a different color?

THE BIRDS

Erasmus: Mmm, I'll bet they each taste pretty much the same!

Charles: [indignant] You wouldn't eat these birds!

Erasmus: Mm, no, I will eat pretty much anything!

Reverend: He is just teasing you, Charles.

Narrator: The reverend turns to Erasmus.

Reverend: Besides, Erasmus, they're too small.

Narrator: Erasmus holds up his hands to indicate a bird about the size of a rabbit. The reverend holds up his hands to indicate a bird the size of a large mouse. Erasmus is disappointed.

Charles: Each of these islands is separated from the others by the ocean water. They all have finches and they all have this one kind of turtle, but from island to island . . .

Reverend: They are different and you cannot explain it.

Erasmus: Frankly, I do not understand why that is interesting.

Charles: It is as if they were once all from the same family of birds, but as they were separated on each island, each changed a little to adapt to its particular island.

Narrator: Thomas rejoins the group. He sets up the cribbage pegs in the board and the doctor shuffles and deals each man a hand of cards. They begin to play the game.

Doc: I did not think that a species of animal would change much over time.

Charles: No one does. Right now we pretty much assume that if an animal is a certain way, then it stays that way.

Doc: That seems reasonable.

Charles: Maybe. Maybe not.

Erasmus: What do you mean maybe not?

Charles: What if you were cutting up meat for tomorrow's stew and there was a sudden wave and you cut off your hand?

Erasmus: I never would cut off my hand, Charles. I've been at sea for half my life already.

Charles: Right, but let's pretend that there is this horrible accident. You would not want to give up your job.

Philosophers to Astronauts Reader's Theater © 2004 Creative Teaching Press

THE BIRDS

Reverend: We would not want him to give up his job. His assistant can barely boil water! We'd starve!

Narrator: The men all laugh.

Charles: Right, so you go on, doing your job, only without your right hand. What happens?

Erasmus: I don't know. I guess I cook with my left hand and get used to it!

Charles: Right. You would adapt.

Erasmus: But it does not make sense for the birds.

Charles: I haven't quite figured it out yet, but to use a similar example, what if the birds arrived on an island where their primary predator would catch them by the legs.

Thomas: What animal catches a bird by the legs?

Doc: None. He's just giving an example of how it works.

Thomas: Oh.

Charles: So one of the birds is born without legs. Normally, that would be a huge problem! But in this case, it is actually an advantage. The bird is not caught by the predator and lives long enough to have baby birds.

Doc: Who do not have legs. So they all live, too.

Charles: And soon, the whole island is filled with legless birds.

Erasmus: Tasty legless birds!

Thomas: I still do not get it. Whoever heard of a legless bird?

Reverend: Explain the real difference you are seeing, Charles.

Charles: In the birds, mostly I am seeing differences in beak shape.

Erasmus: They are paying you to check the shape of birds' beaks?

Charles: No, unfortunately, they are not paying me a thing!

Erasmus: Of course not! What kind of life is that? Charles, you need to develop some skills. Your education is wasted.

Charles: Listen. On one island all the finches have short, rounded beaks. On another, they have long, pointy ones. In all other ways, they are as alike as brother and sister.

THE BIRDS

Erasmus: You know, Reverend, a bird that size might still make a nice shish kebob.

Reverend: [laughing] Be quiet, Erasmus, and let the naturalist explain.

Charles: Why would one beak shape develop on one island and one on another?

Thomas: You do not know that they developed like that. They could have just always been different.

Charles: You are entirely correct, Thomas. The thing that makes me suspicious is that throughout the Galapagos Islands there are always these same birds, each with very, very slight differences. That speaks to a common ancestor.

Charles: So what does a bird do with its beak?

Erasmus: It pecks you, especially if it knows you plan to eat it.

Charles: Stop jibbering and play your hand, Erasmus. The bird eats with his beak. Assuming it has not been caught by a ship's cook, anyway.

Thomas: Can a bird with a short beak eat the same food as a bird with a long beak?

Charles: Not as well, Thomas. A bird with a long, thin beak would find it easier to eat insects in small places like the bark of a tree or hidden in plants. A bird with a short, round beak might do better with seeds or nuts that it has to pick and crack open.

Doc: The long, thin beak might break on the hard shell of the seed.

Erasmus: And the short, round beak could not get inside the cracks of the tree bark!

Thomas: So what exactly are you going to do with the turtles and birds, Charles?

Charles: I am going to study them further. Then perhaps I will write a book about them. I brought some of the turtles onboard with me yesterday.

Erasmus: Ooh, really? Were they in a small, brown box?

Charles: Yes, they were. Why?

Erasmus: Charles, I do not know how to break this to you, so I will give it to you straight. Dinner tonight?

Charles: Yes?

Erasmus: It is turtle stew.

Narrator: There is a moment of silence.

Charles: Well, there are always the birds.

Philosophers to Astronauts Reader's Theater © 2004 Creative Teaching Press

RELATED LESSONS

Habitat Adaptations

OBJECTIVE
Match adaptations to habitats.

ACTIVITY

Divide the class into three groups. Use the following chart to distribute materials to each group. Have them complete the assigned task so they gain an understanding of what their skills and limitations are.

	Materials	**Task**
Group 1	Give each member a **pair of socks,** and have students place a sock on each hand.	Have students use a **clothespin** to pick up another clothespin from the table
Group 2	**Blindfold** every other member of the group. Pair each one with a sighted partner for safety.	Have students walk across the room and pick up a **baseball** (or a similar sized item).
Group 3	Explain to the third group that they cannot use their legs.	Have members of the group lie on the floor and move across the room, pick up a **book,** and transport it back.

Next, give each student a **Habitat Adaptations reproducible (page 50).** Have students read the descriptions of the four habitats and order them based on how well they think their group's adaptation would survive. As a class, discuss the reasons they would do well in their top choice of a habitat.

Darwin, the Man

OBJECTIVE
Gather information about Charles Darwin.

ACTIVITY

Give each student a **Natural Selection reproducible (page 51).** Review the questions on the bottom of the reproducible, and have students set a purpose for reading. Have students read the paragraphs. Then, divide the class into pairs, and have each pair answer the questions. Discuss the answers as a class.

ANSWERS

1. Darwin studied birds on the Galapagos Islands.
2. Darwin studied finches.
3. The finches had different types of beak shapes.

Habitat Adaptations

Directions: Read the descriptions of the following habitats and decide in which habitat your group would have the best chance for survival.

Cave

The cave is dark, which makes it difficult for all the animals to see. Each of the animals must use other senses than sight to find their food source.

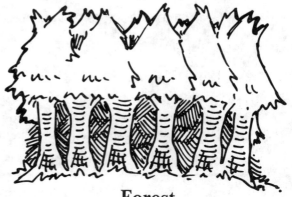

Forest

The forest is filled with trees and small growing plants. Most of the animals that would live here would have to move rapidly to avoid capture.

Swamp

The swamp provides a mix of water and land for animals to move around. Many animals that have short legs or no legs will be able to move rapidly in the water to catch their food and then can move out onto the shore to warm in the sun.

Ocean

The ocean is filled with plants and animals that will attach themselves to rocks to avoid being moved around during the tides. This is a great place to live for animals that have problems moving rapidly or picking up food.

Philosophers to Astronauts Reader's Theater © 2004 Creative Teaching Press

Natural Selection

Directions: Read the passage. Answer the questions on a separate piece of paper.

Charles Darwin talked about how slight differences will allow some members of a group of animals to live while others will die. When he was in the Galapagos Islands, Darwin identified 13 kinds of finches. He figured out that the main difference in the birds was in the beak shape. The different beak shapes helped the birds to eat different foods.

Darwin thought that when the finches first arrived, there was not enough food for all the birds. The birds with slightly different beak shapes could eat other types of food and increase their chances to stay alive, find a mate, and lay eggs. Their chicks would have the same beak shape, be stronger and more able to survive, and have more chicks. The next generation of birds would have more of the new beak shape because the birds with the old beak shape would not be able to find enough food to stay alive long enough to lay eggs.

Darwin thought that after several generations, the birds in that area would all have the new beak shape. This would help them easily get the food they need to survive. The change in the beak shape would then be passed down to future generations and allow the species to survive.

Questions
1. Where did Darwin study the birds?
2. What kind of bird did Darwin study?
3. In what way were the finches different from each other?

JOHN MUIR (1838–1914)

PHILOSOPHERS TO ASTRONAUTS

VOCABULARY

Discuss each of the following words with students. Then, have students identify the word they best understand and least understand. Have volunteers use the word they best understand in a sentence. (You may choose to have more than one example for a given word.)

arachnids: spiders

*****dehydrated:** lacking water; dry

fluid: a gas or liquid

*****glacier:** a large mass of ice in very cold regions or on the tops of high mountains

idle: not wanting to be active; lazy

*****indescribably:** of a quality so great that it cannot be described well in words

prey: an animal hunted by another animal for food

*****torrent:** a fast, heavy stream of water

*used in related activity

BACKGROUND

John Muir was born in Scotland and lived there until about the age of eleven. He attended local schools in Scotland. The family then moved to a rural area of Wisconsin where his extremely strict father allowed little play. John was able to talk his father into allowing him to study on his own by rising at 1 a.m. (after going to bed at 9 p.m.) to read. He was bright and invented accurate, hand-carved clocks, as well as other small inventions. As soon as he was old enough, he left home for college, and from there, he left to travel the United States seeking odd jobs. An industrial accident in his late twenties left Muir blind for over a month and served as a turning point for him. Always interested in nature and the outdoors, he began to travel the world. He walked from Indianapolis, Indiana, to California. Although he continued to travel, he married there and made Northern California his home.

Muir's contribution to science and the world is through his work as a naturalist and writer. He was the driving force behind conservationism at the time and is largely considered the "father" of the national park system. Joseph Cornell, in his award-winning book *John Muir: My Life with Nature* (Dawn Publishing), shares this story:

> Perhaps the greatest (and shortest!) tribute ever given to John Muir was by Reinhold Messner, a German mountaineer. Messner and an American were climbing in the Swiss Alps. The American was surprised to see the Alps so developed, with hotels, villages, and farms dotting the landscape nearly everywhere. He was accustomed to the untouched beauty of the American wilderness, and he asked Messner why the Alps had so many buildings and signs of human activity. With just three words, Messner explained the difference. He said, "You had Muir."

PARTS

Narrator
John Muir: 11-year-old boy
David: 9-year-old brother
Sarah: 13-year-old sister
Anne Muir: mother

FLUENCY INSTRUCTION

Have students discuss the ages of the characters to help them reflect the maturity level in their reading. When you read aloud the script for students, have them listen for the following:

- The entire scene takes place in a very small house at night. The children know they will be strictly punished if they are found awake. Point out that you cannot show emotion by speaking more loudly, but you can drop your voice to a stage whisper.

- Your pace picks up to convey excitement as in the line *John: One in the morning! This is terrific!*

- David is eager to go back to sleep. As the play progresses, your pace slows down when delivering his lines to express sleepiness.

- Your voice rises at the end of a question such as in the line *John: Spiders. I read about spiders. See?*

COMPREHENSION

After you read aloud the script, ask students these questions:

1. At what time of the day does this scene take place?

2. How would you describe John's mother?

3. If you could only do your reading in the middle of the night, what would you choose to read?

4. What is the reason John reads at night instead of during the day?

5. How do you think working all day and reading at night affected the way that John Muir lived as an adult?

A Little Light Reading

PARTS

Narrator
John Muir: 11-year-old boy
David: 9-year-old brother
Sarah: 13-year-old sister
Anne Muir: mother

Narrator: It is dark outside the small frontier house. There are only two bedrooms in this house. The eldest children, Sarah, David, and John, should be fast asleep. Instead, Sarah and David are asleep. John is winding a small clock of his own design.

John: One in the morning! This is terrific!

Narrator: In the large bed next to John, his brother wakes.

David: What are you doing, John? It is the middle of the night! Aren't you tired?

John: I am sore that's for sure!

David: Is that why you cannot sleep? I couldn't believe it when Father said you had to work on digging the new well by yourself today.

John: He needed you in the field. I made some progress. But, no, that is not why I cannot sleep.

David: Maybe you had a bad dream? Blow out the lamp, John. Come to bed!

Narrator: From the bed in the corner of the room comes another sleepy voice.

Sarah: What are you two doing?!? If Father finds out you are up, John, he will surely whip you!

John: No! He said it was OK.

Sarah: Father gave you permission to be out of bed in the middle of the night?

John: I have been begging him for over a month to let me do some reading.

David: He says, "Idle hands are the Devil's tools!"

John: Right. I convinced him that my reading will only help us.

Sarah: How will your books on trees and bugs help us?

John: What do you think ruined that patch of beans?

Philosophers to Astronauts Reader's Theater © 2004 Creative Teaching Press

Sarah: Rabbits. Not trees and bugs. Rabbits.

John: Right. What if I could plant some flowers around the peas that the rabbits can't stand? They would stay away and our peas would be safe!

David: Is there such a thing as a plant that rabbits don't like?

John: Actually, I do not think there is. But the point is still good. If you are going to live in the middle of a forested wilderness, it is helpful to know something about trees.

David: [yawning] Just remember, nobody ever made any money knowing anything about trees.

Sarah: [laughing] As if John cares anything about making money.

John: No, I really don't. Although I think you are wrong, David.

David: About trees and money?

John: Right. You have to know something about trees to grow apples. A man with an apple orchard would make money from knowing something about trees.

David: Fine, then. Is that how you talked Father into it? I would not think he would care about the money either.

John: No, I promised him I would read some from the bible, too.

Sarah: Did you?

John: Sure. Then I read about arachnids.

David: Is that a new kind of vegetable?

John: Spiders. I read about spiders. See? I'm here on the chapter about spiders who hunt other insects.

David: They catch them in a web.

John: No!

Sarah: No?

John: I mean, yes. Yes, some spiders catch flies and gnats and other bugs in webs, but . . . here, look at this picture!

Narrator: John holds up the page for his brother to see.

David: That's disgusting! What is it?

A Little Light Reading

John: Want to see, Sarah? It is a wolf spider! It jumps on its prey and injects a fluid into it.

Sarah: No, thank you. I am afraid it will give me nightmares.

David: Is the fluid poisonous?

John: Worse than that. The fluid actually turns the bug's insides into liquid and then the wolf spider sucks it all out and drinks it.

Narrator: There is silence from all.

Sarah: That is the most disgusting—

David: I cannot believe I am talking to you when Father will have us all up at 5 a.m., and here all you have to talk about—

Narrator: There is a soft noise at the doorway. The children all turn to look in fear. It is their mother. The children sigh with relief.

Children: Phew!

Sarah: I thought we were in big trouble.

Anne: No, but you must be quiet! If you wake your father, he will double your chore load!

John: He said it was OK if I got up to read!

Anne: John, he said it was OK as long as there was no problem with you completing your chores. You may be able to do that, but Sarah and David here will both suffer.

John: I'm sorry, Mother. I will be quiet.

Anne: What are you reading?

John: It is a book about spiders.

David: Arack-knees.

Sarah: Arachnids.

John: Exactly. Spiders.

Anne: Go to sleep, you two.

Sarah: G'night, Mom.

David: 'Night, Mother.

Philosophers to Astronauts Reader's Theater © 2004 Creative Teaching Press

A Little Light Reading

Narrator:	John and his mother continue to talk, but more quietly.
Anne:	Are you sure this is a good idea, John? I just do not see how you will stay awake tomorrow.
John:	Mom, you don't understand. I don't need to be awake to dig a well or plow a field. I just do it. But I'm miserable if that is all I can do! I need a few hours to read and to think.
Anne:	And to dream, I suppose.
John:	When Father gave David and I a few minutes off the other day so we could go explore the woods, I saw so many signs of animals and so many new plants!
Anne:	It was nice of him to let you two do that.
John:	Yes, but it isn't very often. By the time we go back to those woods again, all the things I saw the other day will be gone. Here in the book though are all the answers to the questions I had.
Anne:	Tell me one thing you've learned tonight.
John:	I saw a spider sitting on a leaf. I looked around and there was no web! The spider didn't seem to be interested in building one either. I couldn't figure out how it would catch anything.
Anne:	So you read and found the answer to your question.
John:	Yes.
Anne:	I wonder what you will do with all your natural learning.
John:	Maybe I will write a book like this one!
Anne:	Maybe you will.
Narrator:	She looks at the clock.
Anne:	I hope you will pick an hour more reasonable than 2:00 in the morning to do your writing though!
John:	I don't know . . . it is so nice and quiet!
Anne:	I will leave you to your reading. Tomorrow, before bed, come tell me what you learned.
John:	I will, Mother. Goodnight!
Narrator:	Anne hugs her son, tucks the covers in around David and Sarah, and then heads back to her room. John continues to read by the soft light of the oil lamp.

RELATED LESSON

Rising to the Challenge

> #### OBJECTIVE
> Reflect and write about how a positive attitude can help you overcome a challenge.

ACTIVITY

Give each student the **Joy in the Midst of Hardship** and **Overcoming Challenges reproducibles (pages 59–60)**. Read aloud the passage on the first reproducible, and have students retell where the author is when he is writing, his physical environment, and the challenges that he faces that day. Then, have students read and complete the Overcoming Challenges reproducible.

This activity is adapted from *John Muir: My Life with Nature* by Joseph Cornell (Dawn Publishing). Used with permission of the author. Please see www.sharingnature.com for more information.

Joy in the Midst of Hardship
by Joseph Cornell

John Muir never let cold or wet weather ruin his fun outdoors. When the weather became challenging, Muir said he didn't notice any real discomfort because he was too busy gazing in wonder at the scenery. The following journal entry of Muir's beautifully describes this:

> I was as wet as if I had been swimming after crossing raging torrents and fighting my way through the Alaskan jungle. But everything was deliciously fresh, and I found new and old plant friends, and glacier lessons that made everything bright and light. I saw Calypso borealis, one of my little plant darlings, worth any amount of hardship. And the mosses were indescribably beautiful, so fresh, so bright, and so cheery green. In the evening, I managed to make a small fire out of wet twigs, got a cup of tea, stripped off my dripping clothing, wrapped myself in a blanket and lay thinking on the gains of the day. I was glad, rich, and almost comfortable.

Overcoming Challenges

During John Muir's life, there was no such thing as ultrawarm and light Polartec® fleece, water proof Gore-Tex® clothing, dehydrated camp food, or portable camping stoves. John Muir expected discomfort as he traveled around the world, investigating nature. His positive outlook helped him explore places others would not go and his willingness to tell the world about these places helped him preserve them for future visitors. Describe a time when you made a challenging situation fun by keeping a positive attitude. What happened?

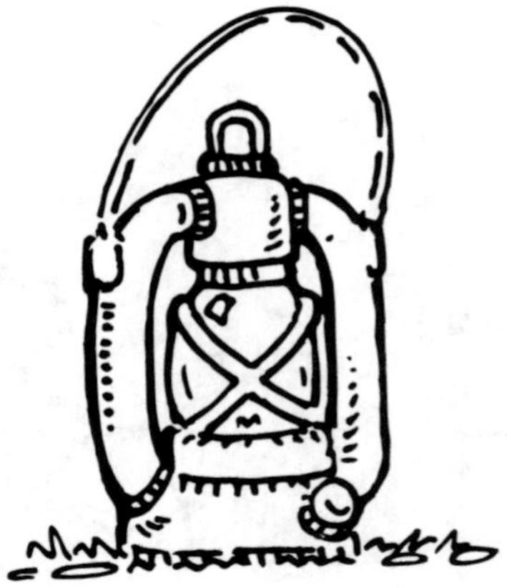

_____

_____

_____

_____

_____

_____

_____

_____

_____

_____

_____

_____

_____

_____

_____

_____

Philosophers to Astronauts Reader's Theater © 2004 Creative Teaching Press

SIR
ALEXANDER
FLEMING
(1881–1955)

PHILOSOPHERS
TO ASTRONAUTS

VOCABULARY

Discuss each of the following words with students. Then, have students discuss how they could learn more about the meaning of each word.

bickering: fighting over petty (little) matters

merciless: without compassion

mold: a fungus that causes organic matter to decay

petrified: frozen in fear

rural: found in or living in the country

wander: to travel without a destination

warren: an underground rabbit home

BACKGROUND

Alexander Fleming grew up the second youngest of eight siblings and half-siblings on a large and very rural Scottish farm. He was extremely bright and later attended school in London. When an uncle left him a small inheritance, he was encouraged to study medicine by his older brother, Tom. All other sibling names here are invented. Alex did not really have any particular interest in microbiology. The events that led to him becoming a bacteriologist had more to do with his fondness for the particular medical school he attended—to become a surgeon as he had originally planned would have meant switching schools. He would one day discover penicillin when a spore from that mold accidentally contaminated a petri dish on which he was growing bacteria. He published a paper on his discovery and then left the work of developing penicillin into the life-saving drug it became to others who had a chemistry background.

PARTS

↯ Narrator
⇡ Alex: 9-year-old boy
  Lucy: 11-year-old sister
  Tom: 12-year-old brother
  Sheila: 14-year-old sister
↯ *Ian: 6-year-old brother

*Ian's lines are numerous,
  but brief.

FLUENCY INSTRUCTION

Have students discuss the ages of the characters to help them reflect the maturity level in their reading. When you read aloud the script for students, have them listen for the following:

- Ian is younger than everyone else. He's excited to be out with all the older kids. He probably speaks more rapidly than the others.
- Sheila is older and acts as a sort of mother to the group. Her voice should communicate that responsibility. Ask students to try a few of her lines to demonstrate how they think they could show that she thinks she is in charge.
- Lucy hisses to quiet the others. Discuss what it means to hiss, and model one way the line **Lucy:** *[hissing] Quiet! There is the mother!* could be read. Invite volunteers to try it.
- A long dash at the end of a line indicates that the speaker is being cut off. Have two volunteers model Ian cutting off Lucy as in the lines **Lucy:** *Honestly, Alex. I am going to bean you. What thing do you see? I only see a big pile of leaves and—* **Ian:** *Look right there.*

COMPREHENSION

After you read aloud the script, ask students these questions:

1. Where does this scene take place?

2. Who is older, Ian or Alex?

3. What was the reason the older kids thought they should not try to catch the rabbits?

4. Who do you think took care of the animals if there was no veterinarian?

5. Why would mold grow better in a damp spot than a dry one?

ICK

PARTS

Narrator
Alex: 9-year-old boy
Lucy: 11-year-old sister
Tom: 12-year-old brother
Sheila: 14-year-old sister
Ian: 6-year-old brother

Narrator: It is mid-afternoon on a rural farm in Scotland. The younger siblings of the large family that owns the farm are wandering through woods on the land. The youngest boy hops up on a rotted log and part of it gives way.

Ian: Aaaah!

Sheila: Are you OK?

Ian: Oh, yes, I'm fine, just a scratch, I think.

Alex: Wow! Look at this! That has got to be the biggest patch of mold I have ever seen on a dead tree log!

All: Ewwww!

Alex: No! Look at it! It is kind of interesting, actually. It's like a plant bruise with its blue and green fuzz . . . there is a gray part there, too.

Sheila: Alex, it is not normal to look at mold that carefully.

Alex: It is not normal to spend a half hour brushing your hair, either, but you did that this morning.

Tom: Stop bickering you two.

Alex: I wonder if I could make the mold grow some more?

Sheila: How, by feeding it some of your lunch?

Alex: No, I thought I would feed it some of your lunch!

Tom: You two are getting boring.

Alex: Fine. I meant by putting it in a damp spot.

Lucy: Why?

ICK

Alex:	Why what?
Lucy:	Why would you want it to grow?
Ian:	Just because it's cool, right Alex?
Alex:	Right, Ian. And because then we would know something else about mold!
Sheila:	Yes, but why would you want to know something about mold?
Alex:	I don't know. Maybe it could come in handy someday. Hey! Look!
Tom:	Now what? Mildew?
Ian:	[whispering, very excited] I see it! I see it!
Tom:	What?!? See what?
Ian and Alex:	Shhh! You will scare it away!
Ian:	No wait! See there?
Alex:	Oh, yes! Yes, I didn't see that before! Good eye!
Lucy:	Honestly, Alex. I am going to bean you. What thing do you see? I only see a big pile of leaves and—
Ian:	Look right there.
Lucy:	There? Oh! Oh, I see now! Oh, how adorable!
Alex:	Adorable? I was thinking maybe for dinner . . .
Sheila:	Stop, Alex! You will make her cry! Gosh, the way you tease is merciless.
Tom:	Show me, then. I can't see what you are all excited about.
Alex:	Right there beneath that log and kind of in the middle of the leaves—see that? A pair of ears?
Ian:	And about a foot away, there are the tips of two more ears sticking out.
Lucy:	They are awfully small, Ian. I don't think they're full grown.
Ian:	I want to see their faces so I will know them if I see them again.
Alex:	All joking aside, Ian, I do not think that is a good idea.
Ian:	We could just move the leaves a little.

Philosophers to Astronauts Reader's Theater © 2004 Creative Teaching Press

Sheila:	Not without giving them a terrible fright. Those two are little. I don't even know what they are doing out of their warren.
Lucy:	Oh, no! What if they're already dead?!?
Tom:	No, no, look. If you watch very carefully the pile of leaves shifts every so often.
Lucy:	Why don't they move?
Alex:	They are probably able to hear us talking very well and they are petrified.
Lucy:	Oh. I still want to see them.
Ian:	Maybe we could spook them a little and they would hop out and we could see them?
Sheila:	What if they got so scared they ran too far and a bigger animal got them?
Narrator:	There is quiet as they all consider the options.
Alex:	Ian, it feels like a wonderful thing, to find these two rabbits, right?
Ian:	Yes!
Alex:	Here we were looking for something else and instead we found this terrific surprise.
Ian:	Exactly.
Alex:	That does not mean it is up to us to spoil their surprise!
Ian:	What surprise?
Alex:	Obviously, they are playing hide-and-seek until their mother comes home.
Lucy:	At which point they will jump out and yell "surprise!"
Tom:	If we scare them now, then the surprise is ruined!
Ian:	Ooohhhh.
Alex:	But, Ian, the rabbits will grow and stay in this area. We can come back as often as you like to see if we can find them again. They'll be older and not as scared of us.
Ian:	OK. I can wait!
Narrator:	Lucy waves her arms frantically.
Lucy:	[hissing] Quiet! There is the mother!
Narrator:	They all begin to whisper to each other.

Philosophers to Astronauts Reader's Theater © 2004 Creative Teaching Press

ICK

Ian: Point to her! I want to see her! Is she gray or brown?

Lucy: She's kind of brown. She blends in beautifully with the leaves. See right there at the bottom of that tree?

Ian: Can I pet *her*?

Lucy, Alex, and Tom: No, Ian.

Tom: You cannot pet her for two reasons, Ian. First, she is a wild rabbit and wild rabbits will sometimes die suddenly when you frighten them.

Alex: Second, if she is sick, and she bites you, you could get sick, too.

Ian: [sulkily] She looks healthy to me.

Tom: Yes, she does. It is very hard to tell what diseases a wild animal has just by looking at it.

Sheila: It isn't as if we could just ask her. That would be nice, wouldn't it?

Ian: Maybe we could take her to an animal doctor?

Sheila: We wouldn't have anybody but Father to take her to. No animal doctors on this farm.

Ian: I am going to be an animal doctor when I grow up then. Like Uncle Tom!

Alex: Uncle Tom is a people doctor, but I am sure that if you wanted to be a veterinarian when you grew up, you would find lots of work.

Ian: Why doesn't she move?

Sheila: She is probably waiting for us to leave so she can go find her babies.

Ian: We should leave then and let the babies surprise her.

Lucy: Good thinking, Ian. I can tell you will make a very good animal doctor.

Alex: Shall we take some of this mold home with us for an experiment then?

Ian: No. That can wait, too.

Sheila: Thank goodness!

Philosophers to Astronauts Reader's Theater © 2004 Creative Teaching Press

RELATED LESSON

Airborne Contaminants

OBJECTIVE
Understand how tiny air impurities may travel.

ACTIVITY

In advance, make a class set of the **Air Contaminants Collector Cards (page 68)** on **card stock.** Explain to students that Alexander Fleming discovered an important bacteria that helped to fight disease when he left a petri dish uncovered in his lab. Spores from the other bacteria traveled through the air, stuck to the surface of the dish, and grew. Explain that there are many kinds of impurities in the air. For example, dust in the air may turn a sunset a pretty red. But too much dust can make us sick. Give each pair of students six **large address labels (at least 2" x 3" or 5 cm x 8 cm),** six **pieces of string,** and a set of six Air Contaminants Collector cards. Have partners write the starting date and time on each card, cut out the cards, trim the cards, and cut the window from each card. Have students center an address label over the open window and stick it to the back of the contamination card. Next, have students tie a piece of string to the card and then hang the cards in various locations throughout the school. After a few days have passed, have students take down each card, carefully record the location on the card, and return to the classroom. Now, give each pair a **magnifying glass,** and have students examine their cards for impurities. Have students share their findings with the class. If time permits, have students record on a **map of the school** areas where they found the greatest evidence of airborn contaminants. Discuss the completed map as a class.

Air Contaminants Collector Cards

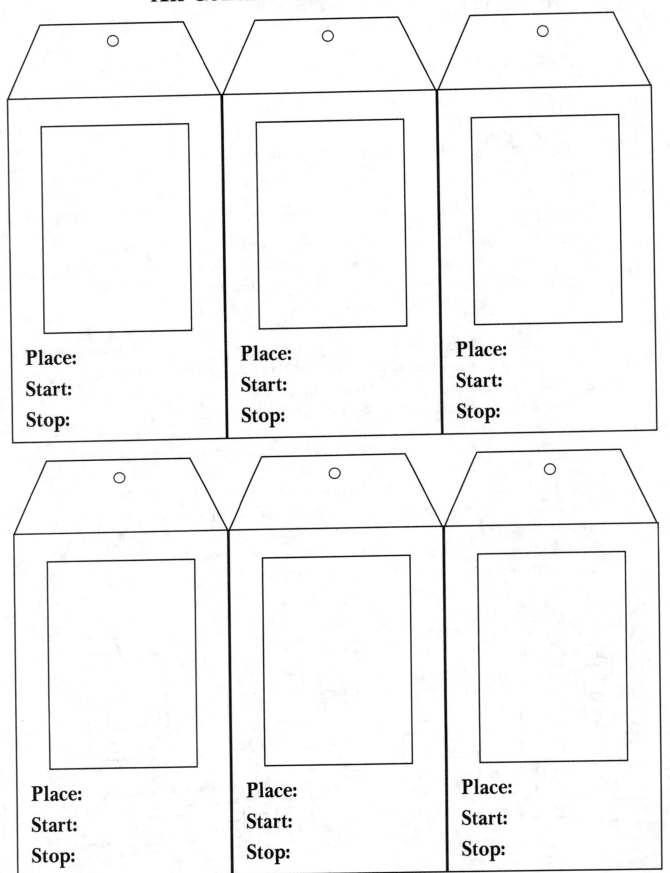

Place:

Start:

Stop:

Place:

Start:

Stop:

Place:

Start:

Stop:

Place:

Start:

Stop:

Place:

Start:

Stop:

Place:

Start:

Stop:

Philosophers to Astronauts Reader's Theater © 2004 Creative Teaching Press

ERNEST JUST
(1883–1941)

PHILOSOPHERS
TO ASTRONAUTS

VOCABULARY

Discuss each of the following words with students. Then, have students sort the words by parts of speech.

appreciate: to understand the value of

convince: to cause a person to believe

expand: to make larger

express interest: to say or show that you are eager about something

focus: a center of activity or interest

realistic: tending to see and accept things as they are

wage: a salary

BACKGROUND

Ernest Just's mother, Mary, acquired several hundred acres of land known as "the Hillsborough Plantation" after her husband died. She founded the town of Maryville, one of the first purely black town governments in South Carolina and a model for blacks throughout the United States. The town was eventually absorbed by the city of Charleston.

Ernest, a student in the school run by his mother, enrolled at the age of thirteen at South Carolina State College in Orangeburg, in the spring of 1896. He completed the normal course in three years and returned to Maryville in 1899, licensed to teach in the black public schools of South Carolina. After a fire burned his mother's school to the ground, his mother decided he should obtain more education and secured his enrollment at Kimball Hall Academy in New Hampshire.

Later, Ernest would go on to attend Dartmouth College, which led to a teaching position at Howard University. He became head of the zoology department and taught through the medical school there. Frustrated by his lack of opportunity in the states, he moved to Europe to work and research there. He had more opportunities and more recognition for his work on cellular structure there. Eventually, poor health sent him back to the states to finish out his life at Howard University. He was 53 years old when he died of cancer. His legacy is his book, *The Biology of the Cell Surface.*

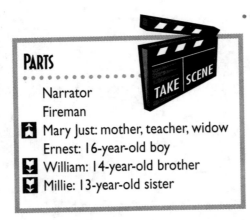

PARTS

Narrator

Fireman

⬆ Mary Just: mother, teacher, widow

Ernest: 16-year-old boy

⬇ William: 14-year-old brother

⬇ Millie: 13-year-old sister

FLUENCY INSTRUCTION

Have students discuss the ages of the characters to help them reflect the maturity level in their reading. When you read aloud the script for students, have them listen for the following:

- The pace of the reading speeds up when children are excited. Have students notice the situation at the start of the scene and point out that the children are excited in a scared way.
- The pace slows down when someone is trying to explain something important to someone else. Have students find one place in the script where this happens.
- Your pace and pitch are fairly steady for any of the narrator lines. These lines usually describe activity and while you avoid monotone, which would be boring, you also avoid conveying too much emotion since the narrator is not part of the scene.
- Your voice pauses for a period, even in the middle of a line such as **William:** *No one speaks Latin, Ernest. Do you really need those classes?*

COMPREHENSION

After you read aloud the script, ask students these questions:

1. What event happened right before the start of the scene?
2. How does that event change Mary's plans for her son's future?
3. Is Ernest interested in going north to school? What lines make you think so?
4. What was the reason Ernest was going to teach for his mother's school?
5. Do you think that he would have been as happy teaching school? Explain your answer.

OPEN DOORS

PARTS

Narrator
Fireman
Mary Just: mother, teacher, widow
Ernest: 16-year-old boy
William: 14-year-old brother
Millie: 13-year-old sister

Narrator: It is early morning in the town of Maryville, South Carolina. Most of the town is still asleep.

Fireman: We still aren't sure what started it, ma'am.

Mary: I guess we will never know.

Narrator: Ernest's younger brother and sister arrive.

Millie: Mama! What happened?

Mary: It looks like a fire started in the kitchen of the school, dear.

Millie: There is nothing left to it!

Mary: It was a small building, Millie. It was entirely in flames by the time we discovered the fire.

Ernest: By the time the firemen got here, the best they could do was water down the ashes.

Mary: All the books and chalkboards that we worked so hard to get for the school are gone. I do not know how we can replace it all!

Millie: Oh, Mother, if anyone can do it, you can!

Fireman: We can help you rebuild, Mary. You started this town. We all know that we are blessed to have you here.

Mary: I appreciate the offer for the help. I know if we decide to rebuild, then we will need many hands on the project.

William: Was anyone hurt?

Mary: No. Even the cat was found hiding at the general store.

Millie: Oh, good!

Ernest: How long will it take us to rebuild, Mother? Will we be able to open in the fall?

OPEN DOORS

Mary: It isn't the school building that will be hard to replace, Ernest. People will pitch in and help us get that back up. It is the books, the chalk, the chalkboards.

Fireman: They could start again with just saying their lessons aloud, Mary. That was how we learned when I was little.

Mary: When I first built the school, Ernest, it was to educate all the children of the new town I founded. Now time has passed and the town has grown. My school is no longer the only school.

Ernest: That is true. Three new schools have opened in the last two years.

Mary: I just don't know if it will be worth it!

Fireman: You can't be thinking of walking away from it! What will Ernest do? You were planning to expand the school and have him take the new class!

Millie: Where will the cat live?

Mary: Oh, heavens, Millie. That cat will do fine anywhere.

William: She'll probably move into the general store and have another litter of kittens under Mr. Roper's counter.

[All laugh.]

Mary: I planned to expand the school and have Ernest take another class, but I have never been convinced that is a good idea, anyway.

Ernest: What do you mean, Mother?

Mary: I think you will be wasting your time and intelligence at our little school, Ernest.

Fireman: What would he do instead?

Ernest: Go north?

Mary: Kimball Hall Academy expressed interest in having you continue there.

William: I want to go, too!

Mary: You are too young. If you apply yourself to your studies as Ernest has, you may be able to go someday, though.

William: What will you study, Ernest?

Philosophers to Astronauts Reader's Theater © 2004 Creative Teaching Press

OPEN DOORS

Ernest: It isn't like college, William. It is a school that prepares you for college. I would study Latin, advanced mathematics, logic, and more.

Millie: I do not think we study much of that. Do we, Mama?

Ernest: Schools for colored children here have very few funds, Millie. We have very few materials. There are entire subjects none of us have had a chance to learn.

William: No one speaks Latin, Ernest. Do you really need those classes?

Ernest: I need the classes to pass the college entrance exams there. I want to go to Dartmouth College, William. And if I want to go into medicine, then yes, I need Latin.

Fireman: Is that a realistic goal, Ernest?

Mary: It is for Ernest. If he can get a good enough education, he can pass any exam he takes with flying colors.

Fireman: It wouldn't be the same as life is here, Ernest. Everyone here knows you and likes you.

Mary: People would be quick to judge, yes, but Kimball Hall Academy would prepare you to go to a real college.

Fireman: South Carolina State College is a real college, Mary.

Mary: He entered at the age of 13 and finished their program in 3 years. It was hardly a challenge.

Fireman: Are there other colored boys at Kimball?

Mary: Not at present, no. I do not know if he would be their first, though. Still, they seem welcoming. I would not send him if I thought he would be in danger.

Ernest: Money will be tight while you recover from the fire, Mother.

Mary: All the more reason you should not stay here. You should get going as soon as we can get you packed.

William: Is it already decided then?

Mary: I feel strongly it is the right decision. Maybe this was meant to happen. Maybe if the school had not burned down, we would have gone on having you teach and the opportunity would have been lost.

Ernest: Mother, I thought we needed my income for the family.

Philosophers to Astronauts Reader's Theater © 2004 Creative Teaching Press

OPEN DOORS

Mary: The school took more money than it made, Ernest. We needed to expand it to keep it going. I can just let it go, now.

Fireman: Then you would just focus on the town government, I suppose.

Mary: Exactly. Charleston is expanding. In another few years, they will absorb our small town. I want to be part of that to try to ease the transition.

Ernest: I would need money for books.

Mary: We will find a way to pay for them.

Ernest: Maybe if I started in New York City. I did hear of some work there the other day. If I could earn a good wage there, then I could send part home and keep the other half for school.

Fireman: You do not need to worry about your mother, Ernest. We won't let anything bad happen to her and the kids. Focus on your studies.

Mary: Besides, it is more expensive there in the city than it is here. I think you may be surprised by the cost. Still, I think the idea of going to New York is a good one.

Millie: Can I help you pack? Will you write? Will you ever come back to visit us?

Ernest: You can help me pack, Millie. Of course I'll write! And I will come back to visit as often as my studies and finances allow.

Fireman: I have to get this crew back to the firehouse and cleaned up, Mary. You have my support with whatever you decide to do. Ernest, I know you will make us all proud whatever you decide.

Ernest: Thank you, sir.

Mary: I am starting to see this as a blessing, son.

Ernest: I do not know if it is a blessing, Mother. I am so sorry you lost your school. But I promise if it is not a blessing, I will work so hard at the Academy that any college in the nation will take me. We will make it a blessing.

Philosophers to Astronauts Reader's Theater © 2004 Creative Teaching Press

RELATED LESSONS

Parts of a Cell

OBJECTIVE
Label the parts of a plant cell and an animal cell.

ACTIVITY
Copy the **Parts of a Cell I reproducible (page 76)** onto an **overhead transparency,** and display it. Explain that Ernest Just helped the world understand more about the parts of cells. His work is important to medicine. Read aloud the cell parts, and talk a little about the parts that are defined for students. If time permits, give each student a copy of the **Parts of a Cell II reproducible (page 77),** and have them color the cells and label the parts.

Ernest Just

OBJECTIVE
Learn more about Ernest Just.

ACTIVITY
Give each student the **Ernest Just** and **Ernest Just Revisited reproducibles (pages 78–79).** Review the questions on the second reproducible, and have students set a purpose for reading. Have students read the paragraphs. Then, divide the class into pairs, and have each pair answer the questions. Discuss the answers as a class.

ANSWERS
1. Ernest Just was born in South Carolina.
2. Maryville had one of the first black town governments.
3. Ernest was 16 years old when he left for Kimball Hall Academy.
4. Ernest was president of the debate club and editor of the school paper at Kimball Hall Academy.
5. Ernest taught at Howard University.
6. Ernest Just is remembered for his work on the structure of cells.

Parts of a Cell I

Animal Cell

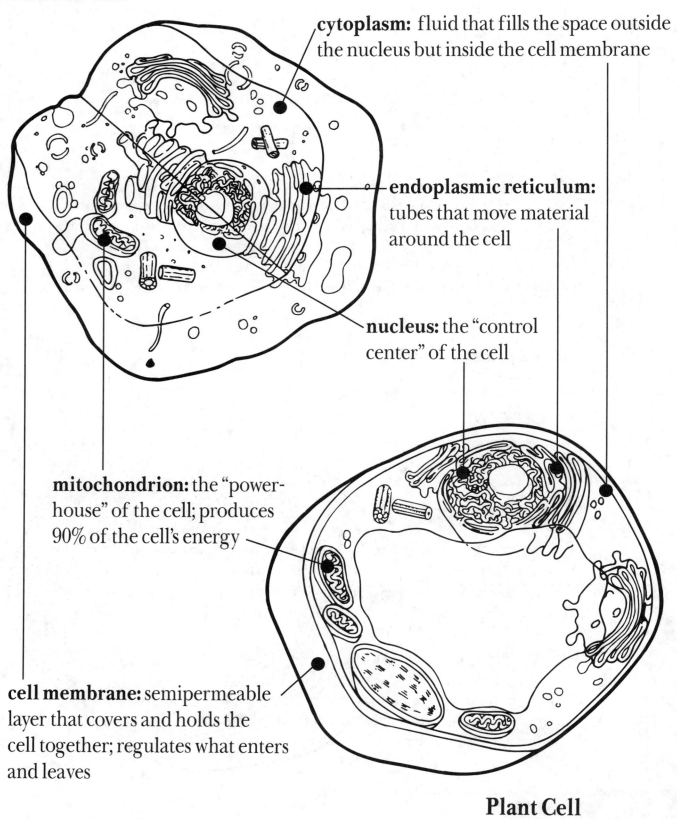

cytoplasm: fluid that fills the space outside the nucleus but inside the cell membrane

endoplasmic reticulum: tubes that move material around the cell

nucleus: the "control center" of the cell

mitochondrion: the "power-house" of the cell; produces 90% of the cell's energy

cell membrane: semipermeable layer that covers and holds the cell together; regulates what enters and leaves

Plant Cell

Parts of a Cell II

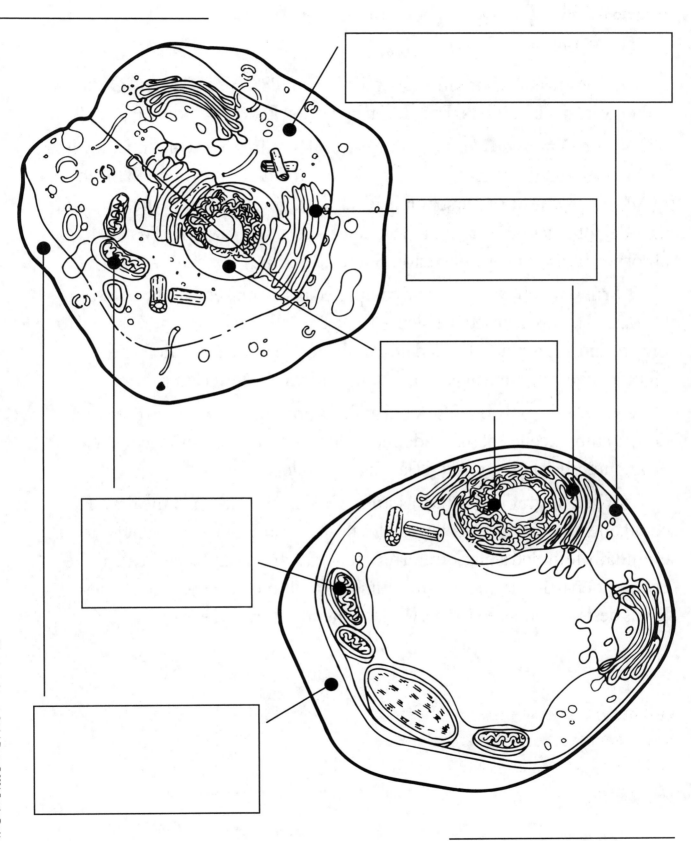

Philosophers to Astronauts Reader's Theater © 2004 Creative Teaching Press

Ernest Just

Directions: Read the passage. Answer the questions on the next page.

Ernest Just was born in South Carolina in 1883. His father and grandfather were dock builders. They both died when Ernest was four years old.

Ernest's mother, Mary, acquired several hundred acres of land known as "the Hillsborough Plantation" after her husband died. She founded the town of Maryville, one of the first purely black town governments in the state and a model for blacks throughout the United States. The town was eventually absorbed by the city of Charleston, South Carolina.

Ernest was only 16 when he completed his formal education in South Carolina. He was licensed to teach. After a fire burned his mother's school to the ground, his mother decided he should obtain more education and secured his enrollment at Kimball Hall Academy in New Hampshire.

He was the only black student at the school, but he was president of the debate club, excelled at his academics, and was the editor of the school paper. From there, he chose to attend Dartmouth College.

When he graduated, he was still limited by the racism of the time. He could only teach in black colleges. He chose Howard University, where he eventually founded a black fraternity, started a drama club, was head of the zoology department, and taught courses in their medical program. Ernest Just is best remembered for his work on the structure of cells.

Philosophers to Astronauts Reader's Theater © 2004 Creative Teaching Press

Ernest Just Revisited

Directions: Read the piece on Ernest Just and answer the questions.

1. Where was Ernest Just born?

2. What was important about Maryville?

3. How old was Ernest when he left for Kimball Hall Academy?

4. Name two things Ernest did at Kimball Hall Academy.

5. At what university did Ernest teach?

6. For what is Ernest Just remembered?

ALBERT EINSTEIN (1879–1955)

PHILOSOPHERS TO ASTRONAUTS

VOCABULARY

Discuss each of the following words with students. Then, have students discuss why each word might be important to understanding the script.

academic: pertaining to school

error: something that is wrong; a mistake

particle: a very small bit or piece of something

petrified: to turn into stone

BACKGROUND

Albert Einstein was the oldest child of a Jewish family in southern Germany. He remained influenced by his faith his whole life. He was sometimes astonished in the way that his ideas about physics were applied to economics (capitalist individualism), religion (relativism), and art (cubism and other modern art). Roger Rosenblatt, an award-winning journalist, says, "He was the first modern intellectual superstar, and he won his stardom in the only way that Americans could accept—by dint of intuitive, not scholarly intelligence and by having his thought applied to practical things, such as rockets and atom bombs."

In this play, only Albert and Elsa are known people. He did spend the last three decades of his life looking for a unified theory, which at the time, was such a daring idea that it was largely considered impossible. He was not successful, but he was eventually vindicated for his efforts as his "problem" is now a focus of quantum physics.

PARTS

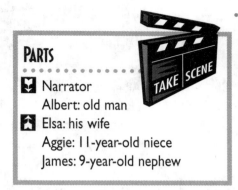

- Narrator
  Albert: old man
- Elsa: his wife
  Aggie: 11-year-old niece
  James: 9-year-old nephew

FLUENCY INSTRUCTION

Have students discuss the ages of the characters to help them reflect the maturity level in their reading. When you read aloud the script for students, have them listen for the following:

- The overall pace of the reading is relaxed. Even the children are in a thoughtful place, working on homework with the help of a doting relative.
- Your pace may sometimes increase when reading the lines where James teases his sister.
- Your pitch falls when you admit confusion as in the line **Aggie:** *I still don't get it.*
- If you want to emphasize a particular part of the line for the listener, pause briefly after the emphasized portion. This will draw attention to what you just said as in the line **Elsa:** . . . *If you change the rules, [pause] you change the particles [pause].*

COMPREHENSION

After you read aloud the script, ask students these questions:

1. Who is Elsa?

2. What are the "large" things in Elsa's explanation?

3. What are the "small" things in Elsa's explanation?

4. Summarize Einstein's question.

5. Do you think that it is important to find the "rules" that govern the universe? Explain your answer.

RESPECT

PARTS

Narrator
Albert: old man
Elsa: his wife
Aggie: 11-year-old niece
James: 9-year-old nephew

Narrator: It is early evening in an older house in New Jersey. An old man with frizzy gray hair and a wild moustache is staring hard at the academic papers in front of him.

Albert: I think you made an error on number nine.

Narrator: The young girl beside him peers over his arm.

Aggie: Nine? Oh. Five plus three is eight, not two.

James: How did you get 2 from that?

Aggie: I subtracted.

Albert: Yes, that kind of thing happens. You set out to do one thing and end up doing the opposite. Here is the eraser.

Narrator: His wife enters the room. She is carrying a tray with glasses of lemonade.

James: Aggie, you need to pay more attention!

Aggie: I was paying attention! I just got mixed up.

James: That's what you told Mama the other day when you put the red scarf in with the white laundry.

Aggie: I did get mixed up. I was putting all the whites on the left and the colored pieces on the right and then I got mixed up.

James: Now we all have pink undershirts.

Elsa: Pink is a nice color, dear.

James: Not for a boy's undershirt!

Elsa: You can color my shirts pink any time you want.

Aggie: No one ever takes me seriously! I don't do these things because I am not paying attention. It is more like I am just paying too much attention to something else!

Albert: What were you paying attention to when you did the wash?

Aggie: I was thinking about the history lesson we had that day and wondering how the Egyptians pulled the very last stone to the top of the pyramid.

Philosophers to Astronauts Reader's Theater © 2004 Creative Teaching Press

RESPECT

James:	What does that have to do with the laundry?
Aggie:	Nothing. Why do I have to think about the laundry?
Albert:	You don't. But if you want to do the laundry well, you probably should try to. Still, I understand how it is to not be able to stop thinking about something that interests you.
James:	Is that why you are famous?
Albert:	I am famous for some things I thought up about twenty years ago.
Aggie:	Do you still think of brilliant things now?
Albert:	[laughing] Not recently. I am thought of as being mostly an old petrified object now. Something that was once wonderful and still fun to dig up and show around at parties, but not very exciting otherwise.
Aggie:	But you haven't stopped thinking. Every time I visit you are scribbling things on paper!
Elsa:	It is his grocery list.
James:	Really?
Elsa:	[laughs] No, I am teasing him. He is thinking very, very hard.
Albert:	Just like you asked yourself a question about the Egyptians, I have asked myself a very large question, and I do not have an answer for it yet.
James:	What is the question?
Elsa:	Let me try to explain it.
Albert:	Go ahead, dear.
Elsa:	In the universe, there are very, very large things in motion.
James:	Like a truck.
Albert:	Use your imagination. These things are much bigger than that.
Aggie:	As big as a skyscraper!
Albert:	A skyscraper is like a particle of sand next to these objects.
James:	A mountain?
Elsa:	Planets. Stars. And they all move around each other.
James:	I know the earth moves around the sun!

RESPECT

Albert: Right, and in space, the sun is moving, too. They all move in a kind of dance.

Aggie: That is nice to think about—the stars dancing.

Elsa: But there are also smaller things.

Aggie: Like a truck!

Albert: [laughing] After the sun, the truck is indeed very small. But think even smaller than that.

James: An ant is very small!

Elsa: Even smaller than an ant.

Aggie: A speck of dirt?

Albert: A speck of dirt is made of millions of these things.

Elsa: We will call them particles.

James and Aggie: Particles.

Elsa: There are rules that govern these particles, too. How they stay together, how they are torn apart, and how they move together. If you change the rules, you change the particles. For example, water and ice are the same particles following the same rules at different temperatures.

Aggie: I don't get it.

James: I think I do. Because water turns to ice when you make it really cold.

Elsa: Right. It hasn't really changed. It is all the same particles. They just act differently, according to their rules, when you change the temperature.

Aggie: I still don't get it.

James: Wait until you are in third grade.

Elsa: The important thing is that these very little things—

Aggie: particles.

Elsa: . . . and the very big things—

James: Planets and stars.

Elsa: . . . all have to follow the rules.

Philosophers to Astronauts Reader's Theater © 2004 Creative Teaching Press

RESPECT

Aggie:	Cool!
James:	But what does that have to do with what Uncle Albert is doing?
Elsa:	Wait, there is one more piece to it. When you are at home, you follow rules set by your parents, right?
James:	Sure!
Elsa:	These rules change from house to house. You follow your parents' rules in their house and the rules of your friend's parents when you go visit a friend. Right?
Aggie:	Right!
Elsa:	Then you go to school and at the school, there is a new set of rules.
James:	Right, like no chewing gum, even though it is OK to chew gum at home.
Elsa:	You understand, good. But both the home and the school have to follow the set of rules of the state or country. Your home cannot set rules that go against the rules of the state. The school cannot set rules that go against the state rules, either.
James:	Right. Even though some of the rules are different, they are all following the rules of the state.
Elsa:	Albert is looking for a set of rules that both the particles and the planets have to follow.
Aggie:	I'll bet there are a lot of people trying to figure out those rules.
Albert:	Actually, there are a lot of people who think the idea is interesting but very few people think the rules actually exist.
James:	So you could be wasting your time.
Albert:	I could be.
Aggie:	But you don't think you are.
Albert:	I think the rules exist. I just do not know if I am the man who will figure them out.
Elsa:	But he is the man who is still trying. No one else is even trying.
Aggie:	And that is what is important, isn't it? Even if other people do not respect your thoughts, what is important is that you go on thinking them.
Albert:	Yes, Aggie. You have it exactly.

RELATED LESSON

Mathematically Speaking

ACTIVITY

Explain that Einstein used logic, imagination, and math to create his theories. Challenge students to use all three of these skills to complete the problems on the **Mathematically Speaking reproducible (page 87).** Have students read each problem, discuss the information they know, and brainstorm ways to solve the problem. After discussing ways to solve the problem, have students use the charts on the **It's a Problem! reproducible (page 88)** to solve the problems. You may want to provide students with linking cubes to help solve the Marbles problem.

ANSWERS

	Mrs. Elvin	Mr. Elvin	Ruthann	Sarah	Alyssa
cheese	x	x	x	x	yes
anchovies	x	x	yes	x	x
sausage	x	x	x	yes	x
peppers	x	yes	x	x	x
mushrooms	yes	x	x	x	x

Hint: Have students graph the given number, 3 yellow marbles. You know that there is an equal number of red marbles. Follow the instructions for each color and graph the results. There are a total of 24 marbles.

9					
8					
7					
6					
5					
4					
3					
2					
1					
	Blue	Red	Yellow	White	Black

Mathematically Speaking

Directions: Read through each problem completely before solving it. Use the charts on the It's a Problem! page to help you solve the problems.

Pizza Pizza!

The Elvin family went out for pizza. They were each going to order a different topping on their pizza. Their favorite toppings are cheese, anchovies, sausage, peppers, and mushrooms. Use the clues to figure out which topping each person had on his or her pizza.

Mrs. Elvin: Doesn't like anchovies or sausage

Mr. Elvin: Likes only green foods

Ruthann: Loves salty fish

Sarah: Does not like vegetables on pizza

Alyssa: Likes cheese

Marbles

Rohit and Linh are sorting their marbles by color. They have twice as many blue marbles as red marbles. They have the same number of red and yellow marbles. There are 2 more white marbles than blue ones. There are half as many black marbles as white marbles. Linh counts 3 yellow marbles. How many of each color marble do they have? How many total marbles?

Philosophers to Astronauts Reader's Theater © 2004 Creative Teaching Press

Name_____   Date _____

It's a Problem!

Directions: Read the problems and use the
information to fill in the charts. The completed
charts should help you solve the problems.

Pizza Pizza!

	Mrs. Elvin	Mr. Elvin	Ruthann	Sarah	Alyssa
cheese					
anchovies					
sausage					
peppers					
mushrooms					

Marbles

9					
8					
7					
6					
5					
4					
3					
2					
I					
	Blue	Red	Yellow	White	Black

Philosophers to Astronauts Reader's Theater © 2004 Creative Teaching Press

KALPANA CHAWLA (1961–2003)

PHILOSOPHERS TO ASTRONAUTS

VOCABULARY

Discuss each of the following words with students. Then, have students identify the word they least understand. Have students research this word and then draw an illustration that clarifies the definition.

envision: to picture in your mind, to dream of

explanation: making something plain or clear

geometry: the area of mathematics that deals with the measurement and relationship of points, lines, angles, plane figures, and solids

thoughtfully: with careful attention or consideration

BACKGROUND

Kalpana Chawla was born and raised in India. Her parents were conservative and religious, but Kalpana was the youngest of her siblings and was able to convince her parents to let her do things normally not permitted for girls. She enjoyed activities like karate and looked up to her older brother, who wanted to be a jet pilot. She was an exceptional student and eventually came to the United States to study aerospace engineering. She met and married an American flight instructor. Kalpana Chawla was the first Indian-born astronaut. She died when the space shuttle, *Challenger*, broke up over the skies of southern Texas. In this play, she walks to school with her older siblings. Montu was her childhood nickname. The names of her siblings are accurate, but their ages have been estimated.

PARTS

♦ Narrator

♦ Montu (childhood nickname of
   Kalpana Chawla): 9-year-old girl
Sanjay: 12-year-old brother
Sunita: 14-year-old sister
Deepa: 11-year-old sister

FLUENCY INSTRUCTION

Have students discuss the ages of the characters to help them reflect the maturity level in their reading. When you read aloud the script for students, have them listen for the following:

- The pace of the reading speeds up when children are excited. Have students name at least three places where the reading pace will pick up in this script.

- The pace slows down when someone is being earnest. Have students notice how carefully you enunciate and pace your words when you speak Montu's line addressed to her sisters: **Montu:** *When you look in the sky, and you know that you could fly there if you had the right plane and the right lessons, don't you want to go?*

- Your pitch is ever so slightly lower for the older daughter Sunita. Point out that Deepa and Montu are younger than Sunita and the actors with those roles will need to find a way to show that with their voices.

COMPREHENSION

After you read aloud the script, ask students these questions:

1. Which character is Kalpana Chawla in the scene?

2. What are some ways she likes to spend her free time?

3. What does Montu want to be when she grows up? Why?

4. Would you want to fly in space if you had the opportunity? Explain your answer.

5. Do you think that her family supported her becoming an astronaut? Why or why not?

FLYING

PARTS

Narrator
Montu (childhood nickname of
    Kalpana Chawla): 9-year-old girl
Sanjay: 12-year-old brother
Sunita: 14-year-old sister
Deepa: 11-year-old sister

Narrator: It is a bright, sunny day in early spring. A group of children is walking to school. It is India and it is 1971. A young girl runs up to join the others.

Montu: Phew! That was close. I almost forgot my uniform. You know, it is the weirdest thing. It is never where I left it!

Deepa: Maybe if you cleaned your side of the room a little more often . . .

Sanjay: No, I think Mom hides it on purpose.

Sunita: [laughing] Oh, probably.

Montu: Why would she do that?

Sanjay: You know, little sister. She just thinks there are better ways for a girl to spend her time than to take a karate class!

Narrator: Montu tilts her head thoughtfully.

Montu: But she said it was OK!

Sunita: You pester Mom and Dad so much that sooner or later they always say, "Yes."

Deepa: [teasing] But Mom, please, it is just this one thing!

Sanjay: And soon you are taking karate, climbing trees, running races, entering the science fair . . .

Sunita: And practically always the only girl.

Narrator: Montu grins. She does not really think there is anything wrong with this.

Montu: Daddy always fusses. He wants to be so strict. But in the end, if you say, "Please! I want it!" often enough . . .

Sunita: He always gives in to you.

Deepa: It is because you are the baby!

Montu: It is because he does not really mind.

Sanjay: None of us really mind. It is fun to watch all the things you do.

Montu: So you are coming to see me test for my next belt this afternoon?

Sunita and Sanjay: Yes!

Deepa: I can't. I promised to help our neighbor watch her kids so she could sew her sister's wedding dress.

Montu: I will tell you all about it tonight after we are in bed.

Deepa: But I want you to help me with my math after dinner, OK? I have a test tomorrow.

Sanjay: Why is Montu helping you with your math? She is two grades below you. I can help!

Montu: It is just some geometry. I just read her book and explain it to her.

Deepa: She just gets it faster than I do and her explanation makes so much more sense than whatever is in the book.

Sanjay: What will you learn when you are in Deepa's grade?

Montu: Maybe they would let me skip it!

Sanjay and Sunita: No, I don't think so.

Montu: But I could try . . .

Sanjay and Sunita: No, I don't think so.

Montu: But—

Sanjay and Sunita: No!

Sanjay: Don't be in such a hurry, little sister. You are very smart and you are very good at the things you do.

Sunita: I am sure you will do well tonight and get your next karate belt.

Sanjay: But if you are patient and take your time, you can probably go further than Mom and Dad even envision for you right now.

Montu: All they want for me is a good husband.

Deepa: All I want for me is a good husband! Why is that bad?

Philosophers to Astronauts Reader's Theater © 2004 Creative Teaching Press

FLYING

Sunita: It is not bad, it is good, but Montu wants other things, too.

Deepa: She can have them. I want what mother has. A good husband, a good home, and four good kids.

Sunita: Sure, and you will have those things, Deepa. But you have to admit that Montu is different.

Montu: I am not that different!

Sanjay: What do you want to be when you grow up, Montu?

Montu: A pilot! Just like you do.

Sunita: Montu, how many other girls in your class also want to be pilots?

Narrator: Montu thinks about it.

Montu: Probably it just did not occur to them yet that they could be a pilot.

Deepa: Honestly, Montu. Probably it never will occur to them that they want to be a pilot.

Montu: When you look in the sky, and you know that you could fly there if you had the right plane and the right lessons, don't you want to go?

Sunita and Deepa: No.

Sunita: But you do. Why is that? It is just because Sanjay does?

Montu: No! I mean, I like to talk to Sanjay about it because he understands, but I don't want to fly because of him. I want to fly because of what is in my heart.

Deepa: Montu, you are so young. How can you really know what is in your heart?

Sunita: It is so dangerous, Montu! You should be afraid.

Deepa: I think you lack fear because you do not know the risks you are taking, not because you want so much to fly.

Montu: No, Deepa, you are wrong. I mean, I am certain I have a lot to learn about flying, but I do know some of the dangers! Men and women who fly and make mistakes—sometimes they don't get a chance to learn from them. It is over.

Sunita: What if you made a mistake like that? What would happen to Mom and Dad?

Deepa: Mother would never forgive herself for allowing you to go.

FLYING

Sanjay: You are trying to guilt her out of her passion. And anyway, you are wrong. If Montu succeeds in learning to fly, Mother will know she did it to make her dreams come true.

Montu: I do not want to die in an airplane. I want to fly one! Is it dangerous? Yes! But—

Narrator: She stops her siblings and gestures for them to look at the sky.

Montu: Up there you can see all of the world's people moving about like tiny ants and they all look equal. They all do their part for the world. Up there you can see the Ganges Valley and the Himalayan Mountains and it is not through a television set or from 4 feet high, but from the sky.

Sanjay: It would make your heart almost stop to see those things . . .

Montu: . . . to have those things that fill your dreams instead fill your eyes.

Narrator: There is a moment of silence.

Deepa: You will need to go to the university then.

Sunita: Oh my, I do not want to be around when you have that conversation with Father.

Sanjay: I will feel sorry for the other students then.

Montu: For having to study with a girl? Are you against me, too?

Sanjay: No, for having to study with a classmate so much smarter than they are. Someday, Montu, I will fly jet planes.

Montu: To break the sound barrier!

Sanjay: Will you be my co-pilot?

Montu: Only if you let me drive sometimes!

Sanjay: It's a deal, little sister.

Philosophers to Astronauts Reader's Theater © 2004 Creative Teaching Press

RELATED LESSONS

A Day in Her Life

OBJECTIVE

Imagine and write about a day in the life of an astronaut.

ACTIVITY

Write the writing prompts shown below on the board. Have students choose one for a writing topic. Provide additional time for editing and a final draft. After students have completed their responses, invite students to read their work to the class.

1. The space station has changed dramatically since the first astronaut went into space in 1961. Write a short story involving space travel in the future.

2. NASA subcontracts with many companies. Think up a product that would be useful to NASA. Write a letter to NASA encouraging them to buy the product.

3. Helmets and space suits are an important part of space travel. They protect the astronaut! Design a new space suit with features for everything an astronaut could want or need. Describe your suit in your paper.

The International Space Station

OBJECTIVE

Learn more about the International Space Station.

ACTIVITY

Give each student **The Space Station reproducible (page 96).** Review the questions on the bottom of the reproducible, and have students set a purpose for reading. Have students read the paragraphs. Then, divide the class into pairs, and have each pair answer the questions. Discuss the answers as a class.

ANSWERS

1. This piece is about the International Space Station.
2. The space station is designed to conduct important experiments.
3. Japan is providing one of the labs for the space station.

The Space Station

Directions: Read the passage. Answer the questions on a separate piece of paper.

Sixteen nations participated in the building of the International Space Station. Each space agency of the various countries took responsibility for building a part of the station. The space station is the greatest peacetime international collaboration ever attempted and is designed to allow scientists to conduct research and long-term experiments in space.

The space station will eventually be more than four times as large as the Russian Space Station Mir. It will have over an acre of solar panels to provide power and be 360 feet by 290 feet (109.7 m by 88.4 m).

The United States is managing the project and providing some of the most important elements of the space station such as life support and temperature control. Canada is contributing a 55-ft (16.8-m) robotic arm for assembly and maintenance tasks. The European Space Agency is providing a lab for the station. Japan is also making a lab for the station. Russia, Brazil, and Italy are providing the rest.

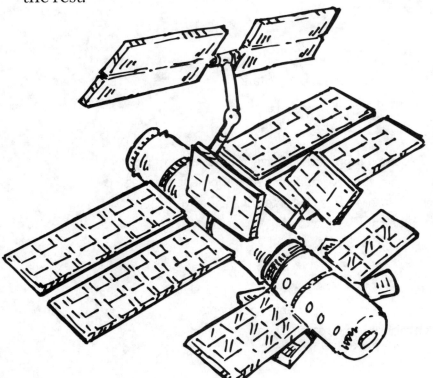

Questions
1. What is this piece about?
2. What is the purpose of the space station?
3. What is Japan making for the space station?

Philosophers to Astronauts Reader's Theater © 2004 Creative Teaching Press